TECHNICAL REPORT

Using Social Media to Gauge Iranian Public Opinion and Mood After the 2009 Election

Sara Beth Elson • Douglas Yeung • Parisa Roshan • S. R. Bohandy • Alireza Nader

RAND NATIONAL SECURITY RESEARCH DIVISION

This publication results from the RAND Corporation's Investment in People and Ideas program. Support for this program is provided, in part, by the generosity of RAND's donors and by the fees earned on client-funded research.

Library of Congress Cataloging-in-Publication Data

Using social media to gauge Iranian public opinion and mood after the 2009 election / Sara Beth Elson ... [et al.].
p. cm.
Includes bibliographical references.
ISBN 978-0-8330-5972-7 (pbk. : alk. paper)
1. Presidents—Iran—Election—2009—Public opinion. 2. Public opinion—Iran. 3. Social media—Political aspects. 4. Social media—Political aspects—Research. I. Elson, Sara Beth.

JQ1789.A5U75 2012
324.955'061—dc23

2011049687

Cover image courtesy of Jose Luis Pelaez Inc. (Blend Images/Getty Images)

Published 2012 by the RAND Corporation
1776 Main Street, P.O. Box 2138, Santa Monica, CA 90407-2138
1200 South Hayes Street, Arlington, VA 22202-5050
4570 Fifth Avenue, Suite 600, Pittsburgh, PA 15213-2665
RAND URL: http://www.rand.org/
To order RAND documents or to obtain additional information, contact
Distribution Services: Telephone: (310) 451-7002;
Fax: (310) 451-6915; Email: order@rand.org

Preface

The role of social media in the protests following the 2009 Iranian presidential election has been widely reported. This report presents an analysis of Iranian public opinion and mood as expressed over Twitter in the nine months following the election. The research represents an initial case study of a novel methodology developed to analyze politically oriented social media content. In addition to policy-relevant findings regarding Iranians' attitudes toward a variety of topics (e.g., President Mahmoud Ahmadinejad, Supreme Leader Ali Khamenei, the United States), our methodological approach is described in detail. The results should be of interest to analysts and policymakers concerned with Iranian politics and public opinion in closed societies, as well as social media researchers.

This paper is a product of the RAND Corporation's continuing program of self-initiated independent research. Support for such research is provided, in part, by donors and by the independent research and development provisions of RAND's contracts for the operation of its U.S. Department of Defense federally funded research and development centers. The research was conducted within the International Security and Defense Policy Center of the RAND National Security Research Division (NSRD) of the RAND Corporation. NSRD conducts research and analysis on defense and national security topics for the U.S. and allied defense, foreign policy, homeland security, and intelligence communities and foundations and other nongovernmental organizations that support defense and national security analysis.

For more information on the International Security and Defense Policy Center, see http://www.rand.org/nsrd/ndri/centers/isdp.html or contact the director (contact information is provided on web page).

Contents

Preface ... iii
Figures and Table ... ix
Summary ... xi
Acknowledgments ... xix
Abbreviations ... xxi

CHAPTER ONE
Introduction ... 1
Analysis of Social Media Can Help Gauge Public Opinion and Mood in Closed Societies ... 2
A New Computer-Based Tool Offers a Promising Means of Tapping into Politically Oriented Content in Social Media ... 2
This Type of Analysis Can Have Important Policy Uses ... 3
Organization of This Report ... 4

CHAPTER TWO
Methodology ... 5
The Precedent for Our Approach: Previous Research Using LIWC and Word-Usage Analysis ... 5
LIWC Has Been Shown to Accurately Represent Verbal Expression ... 5
The Real Potential of Exploring Word Usage Lies in Its Links with Behaviors and Outcomes ... 5
Word Usage Is Now Being Studied in Politically Oriented Contexts ... 6
Our Research Process ... 6
Planning Tasks: Understanding the Sphere of Relevant Social Media ... 7
Selecting Twitter Texts ... 7
Selecting Iran-Relevant Political Topics ... 8
Selecting the LIWC Word Categories to Use in Our Analysis and Defining How We Would Interpret Them ... 8

CHAPTER THREE
Background on Social Media Use in Iran and Events Surrounding the 2009 Election ... 11
Social Media Use in Contemporary Iran ... 11
The Scale of Internet and Social Media Usage in Contemporary Iran ... 11
Who Is Using Social Media in Iran? ... 12
The Anonymity Factor ... 12
The Iranian Information Environment Prior to the 2009 Presidential Election ... 13
The Use of Social Media During the 2009 Presidential Election in Iran ... 14

The Role of Social Media in Iran's Internal Politics Grew Rapidly After the 2009 Presidential Election ... 15
Major Events in Iran During the Post-Election Period ... 17
The Rise of Mass Protests ... 17
June 19: Khamenei's Friday Prayer Speech ... 18
June 20: Neda Agha-Soltan's Death ... 18
July 9: Anniversary of the 1999 Student Uprisings ... 18
August 5: Ahmadinejad's Inauguration ... 19
September 18: Quds Day ... 19
Late December: Ashura Day Protests ... 20
February 11, 2010: 31st Anniversary of the Islamic Revolution ... 20

CHAPTER FOUR
Overall Trends in Public Mood in Iran After the 2009 Presidential Election ... 23
Public Mood Throughout the Nine Months After the Election ... 23
Twitter's Clearest Indicator of Mood and Forecaster of Action: Swear Words ... 23
Use of Pronouns on Twitter After the Election ... 25
Summary ... 28

CHAPTER FIVE
Iranian Public Opinion About Specific Topics in the Aftermath of the 2009 Election ... 29
Public Opinion Leading Domestic Political Figures: Ahmadinejad, Khamenei, Mousavi, and Karroubi ... 29
Summary ... 29
Background ... 30
Comparing Trends in Public Opinion About Political Figures ... 31
Around the Quds Day Protest, Twitter Users Wrote More Negatively About Khamenei Than About Ahmadinejad ... 31
At Certain Points, Twitter Users Wrote More Positively and Less Negatively About Karroubi Than About Mousavi ... 33
Initially, Twitter Users Swore More About Ahmadinejad Than About Mousavi, but the Opposite Became True ... 36
Policy Implications ... 37
Pro-Government and Opposition Groups: The Green Movement, the Revolutionary Guards, and the Basij ... 38
Summary ... 38
Background ... 38
Comparing Trends in Public Opinion About Political Groups ... 39
The Green Movement Was Viewed More Positively Than the Revolutionary Guards or Basij ... 39
Twitter Users Swore More About the Basij Than About the Revolutionary Guards ... 40
Public Opinion About the United States, President Obama, and the CIA ... 42
Summary ... 42
Usage of Swear Words Suggests Early Frustration with the United States and President Obama, as Well as a Strong Desire for U.S. Action ... 43
Usage of First-Person Singular Pronouns Regarding the United States and President Obama Generally Paralleled Usage of Swear Words ... 46

Pronoun Use When Writing About Obama as Compared with Iranian Figures 48
Twitter Users Expressed Less Negative Emotion When Writing About Obama as Compared with Iranian Figures 50
Positive Emotions in Tweets About Obama Showed Several Pronounced Spikes Compared with Tweets About the United States 52
Some Twitter Users Pointed to Foreign Influence, Particularly Intelligence Agencies, as the Driving Force Behind Protests 53
Public Opinion About Specific Countries: Israel, the United States, and Iran 55
Summary 55
Twitter Users Only Infrequently Swore Regarding Israel or the United States 56
Twitter Users Swore More When Referring to the "Islamic Republic" Than to "Iran" 57
Twitter Users Expressed Positive Emotions Toward Israelis Who May Have Aided the Protest Movement 58

CHAPTER SIX
Methodological Considerations 61
Additional Demonstration of the Methodology: Sadness Words 61
Linguistic Indicators That Did Not Work as Expected on Twitter 62
Differences in Phrasing May Reflect Differing Intentions and Writing Styles 63
Limitations of Automated Analysis Suggest That It Is a Complementary Approach to Manual Analysis 65

CHAPTER SEVEN
Next Steps: A Design for a Second Phase of This Program of Research 67
Looking Ahead Toward the 2013 Iranian Presidential Elections 67
Validating the Methodology 68
Improving Current Aspects of the Methodology 69
Expanding the Scope of the Current Work 70

APPENDIX
Additional Details Regarding Methodology: Data Collection and Analysis 73

References 79

Figures and Table

Figures

S.1. Rates of Swearing on Twitter After the 2009 Presidential Election xvi
4.1. Swearing om Twitter After the Election 24
4.2. Usage of First-Person Singular and Second-Person (Singular and Plural) Pronouns on Twitter After the Election 26
5.1. Comparing Usage of "Anxiety" Words When Writing About Khamenei and Ahmadinejad 32
5.2. Comparing Usage of First-Person Singular Pronouns When Writing About Khamenei and Ahmadinejad 33
5.3. Comparison of Swearing About Khamenei and Ahmadinejad Over Time 34
5.4. Comparison of Positive-Emotion Expressions for Karroubi and Mousavi Over Time 35
5.5. Comparison of Swearing About Mousavi and Karroubi Over Time 36
5.6. Comparison of Swearing About Ahmadinejad and Mousavi Over Time 37
5.7. Expression of Positive Emotions in Connection with the Green Movement, IRGC, and Basij 40
5.8. Swearing About the IRGC and Basij After the 2009 Election 41
5.9. Comparison of Swearing When Writing About the United States and Obama 44
5.10. Usage of First-Person Singular Pronouns When Writing About the United States and Obama 47
5.11. Usage of First-Person Plural Pronouns When Writing About Obama and Ahmadinejad 49
5.12. Usage of First-Person Plural Pronouns When Writing About Obama and Mousavi 50
5.13. Usage of First-Person Singular Pronouns When Writing About Obama and Ahmadinejad 51
5.14. Usage of First-Person Singular Pronouns When Writing About Obama and Mousavi 52
5.15. Comparison of Sadness Words When Writing About Obama, Khamenei, and Ahmadinejad 53
5.16. Comparison of Anxiety When Writing About Obama, Khamenei, and Ahmadinejad 54
5.17. Usage of Positive-Emotion Words When Writing About the United States and Obama 55
5.18. Comparison of Swear Words When Writing About the "Islamic Republic" and "Iran" After the 2009 Election 57
5.19. Usage of Positive-Emotion Words When Writing About Israel After the 2009 Election 59
6.1. Patterns in Sadness Expressed on Twitter After the Election 61
6.2. Seeming Patterns in Sadness Expressed When Writing About Karroubi and Mousavi 63

6.3. Seeming Patterns in Positive Emotion Expressed When Writing About Ahmadinejad and Mousavi 64
6.4. Seeming Patterns in Anxiety Expressed When Writing About Karroubi and Mousavi 65

Table

S.1. Word Categories Indicating Public Opinion and Mood and How We Interpreted Them xiv

Summary

In countries where freedom of expression is limited, social media, such as Twitter, blogs, and Facebook, are playing an increasingly visible role in politics. For example, in the absence of democratic elections, an estimated 70 million bloggers in China have become the *de facto* voice of the people (Friedman, 2010). In another example, an increasing number of Pakistanis turned to YouTube, Flickr, Facebook, and Short Message Service (SMS) text messages as alternative media portals during the 2007–2008 "Pakistan Emergency," which began after Pakistan's president, General Pervez Musharraf, suspended the Chief Justice of the Supreme Court, and the government jammed cell phone networks and blocked news channels (Yusuf, 2009). And finally, in the months after the contested Iranian presidential election in June 2009, Iranians blogged, posted to Facebook, and, most visibly, coordinated large-scale protests on Twitter. Twitter users sent tweets—short text messages posted using Twitter—marked with the "IranElection" hashtag (i.e., labeled as being about the Iran election) at a rate of about 30 new tweets per minute in the days immediately following the election.

The use of social media in closed societies such as Iran's—where people's freedom of expression is curtailed—presents a novel opportunity for analysts to gain insight into public opinion and mood where previously they faced significant barriers. Analysts studying public opinion in open societies have multiple tools at their disposal: face-to-face surveys, on-site observation, media analysis, and telephone poll results. But the inherent nature of a closed society makes it difficult, and sometimes impossible, for analysts to apply these methods, which require people to cooperate openly and media to be uncensored. In contrast, social media, because they can be used in anonymity, offer an alternative to which numerous people in closed societies are turning in lieu of making public or traceable statements. As such, they offer analysts an alternative source of data on public opinion and mood in places where people may fear retribution for expressing themselves freely.

Computer-Based Analysis: A Promising Counterpart to the More Established Approach to Analyzing Social Media

At present, analysts typically use a "manual" approach to study the content of social media. For example, they might read a few select blogs or follow a specific set of people on Twitter. Then, they interpret the postings they read and, typically, present their analysis in a report. The manual approach can provide analysts with an in-depth understanding of posted content, allowing them to interpret the nuance, subtlety, and implicit meanings inherent in what people write. However, it also has significant drawbacks. Analysts may read the wrong material. They are constrained by the amount of text they can read in a given workday. It will be impossible for them to gain an understanding of public opinion or mood on a mass scale. And analysts' biases may affect their interpretations of what they read.

Given the shortcomings of the manual approach, using a computerized method to study the content of social media can serve as a useful complement, compensating for some of these limitations. Such a tool exists: an automated content analysis program called "Linguistic Inquiry and Word Count 2007" (LIWC, pronounced "Luke") (Pennebaker, Booth, and Francis, 2007; Pennebaker et al., 2007). Able to analyze thousands of social media posts in only a few seconds, LIWC offers a number of advantages. For instance, analysts can gain a bird's-eye view of what people are saying and feeling across many social media sites over time. Analysts can also quantify their data, in this way reducing the chance that their biases affect their interpretations of social media texts. Ultimately, combining an automated approach with the more traditional, manual approach is most likely to yield optimal results.

However, LIWC is largely untested in political contexts. In the past, researchers have used LIWC in a variety of ways—for example, to study language patterns after traumatic events (Gortner and Pennebaker, 2003; Stone and Pennebaker, 2002), to investigate how men and women communicate differently (Newman et al., 2008), and to detect deception (Hancock et al., 2008; Newman et al., 2003). But LIWC has not been widely applied to understanding a non-Western political context.

Recognizing the potential of this computer-based tool to shed light on public opinion in closed societies, we tested LIWC by applying it to the case of Iran. Focusing on Twitter, we used LIWC as a means of tapping into Iranian public opinion and mood during the tumultuous months following the highly controversial 2009 presidential election. The post-election period may be viewed as extending from the election itself in 2009 until major protests ended nine months later, in February 2010. With this period as our focal point, we examined

- how Twitter users tweeting about the election felt, in general, over these nine months
- whether their sentiments tracked with the outbreak of protests
- how they felt about political leaders, including Supreme Leader Ali Khamenei, President Mahmoud Ahmadinejad, opposition presidential contenders Mir Hussein Mousavi and Mehdi Karroubi, and U.S. President Barack Obama
- how they wrote about certain groups affiliated with either the Iranian government or the opposition, including the Islamic Revolutionary Guards Corps (IRGC), the Basij paramilitary force, and the Green Movement
- how they wrote about certain countries, including the United States, Israel, and Iran.

Given that LIWC is largely untried in non-Western political contexts, we used Iran during this period as a test case. On the one hand, we sought to shed light on how public opinion and mood evolved after the 2009 election. But at the same time, we intended to examine the validity of a new methodology—one incorporating the LIWC tool—for analyzing foreign public sentiment on political topics, as expressed through the social media platform, Twitter.

How Does LIWC Work?

LIWC was developed to analyze the characteristics and patterns of written text, allowing one to draw conclusions about people's psychological states (e.g., emotions, desire for social interaction) on the basis of their usage of specific categories of words. LIWC contains approximately 80 such categories: first-person singular pronouns, positive emotion words, and swear words are three examples. For a given text, LIWC first counts the total number of words in that text. Then it searches for all words contained within each of the 80 categories, keeping tally of the number of instances in each category. Each time LIWC encounters a word in a given category, it increments that category by one. Finally, LIWC calculates a ratio of the number of words within each category divided by the total number of words in the text.

Such LIWC-generated ratios (the quantitative data) can then be interpreted qualitatively, by using established research linking the use of specific words to psychological states and behaviors. On this basis, by examining, for example, how large or small the ratios are or how they change over time, one can gain insight into how widely felt certain implicit sentiments are among a group of people or examine how their opinions and sentiments have shifted.

Ample Precedent for Using Word-Usage Analysis to Assess Public Opinion

A strong precedent exists for using LIWC in this way, in the form of previous research that has connected people's use of certain word categories with their emotions, attitudes, and behaviors. For example, greater use of first-person singular pronouns—talking and thinking about oneself—has been shown to suggest feelings of depression (Rude, Gortner, and Pennebaker, 2004) and poor coping with traumatic events. Second-person or plural pronouns indicate reaching out to others (Chung and Pennebaker, 2007) and a sense of community or group identity. (These words are typically used more frequently around large-scale, shared traumas [Cohn, Mehl, and Pennebaker, 2004; Gortner and Pennebaker, 2003; Stone and Pennebaker, 2002].) Validations of LIWC suggest that it accurately characterizes emotions in written language (Kahn et al., 2007) and that the results it generates are comparable to those produced with other content-analysis methods (Alpers et al., 2005). In addition, LIWC has been successfully applied more recently to various forms of social media (e.g., blogs) (Pennebaker et al., 2007).

Our Approach to the Analysis

Our computer-based methodology centered on examining the rates at which people posting on Twitter about the Iran election used certain categories of words. To interpret the attitude or emotion conveyed by these categories, we used established precedent from the LIWC literature. We then (1) tracked the rates of use over the nine-month period following the 2009 Iranian presidential election and (2) examined whether patterns in these rates coincided with political events, to gain insight into how people may have felt before, during, and after those events.

Collecting and Preparing the Sample

We began by selecting a set of relevant Iranian political topics to analyze using LIWC. Next, we constructed an automated software program to parse and clean the social media texts in our sample, and we stored the texts in a database. We analyzed 2,675,670 tweets marked with the "IranElection" hashtag,[1] posted by 124,563 distinct individuals and dated from June 17, 2009, to February 28, 2010. As this hashtag was 2009's second most popular topic across all of Twitter (Twitter Blog, 2009b), this set of data should provide broad coverage of the election discussion among Twitter users. This sample necessarily included observers throughout the world, as well as people in Iran, who were all communicating with each other. In addition, all of the tweets in this dataset were written in English. But a review of many of them (shown below as they appeared) suggested that their authors were Iranians living inside Iran:

> Just went to Vanak square site of previous protests. All calm so far
>
> oh my dear god please help us. no one helping us but we still fighting the Basij.
>
> We been beaten tortured and killed for 30yrs! Nothing the SUPREME LIAR says can break our will![2]

Processing and Interpreting the Data

We then processed the data with LIWC and conducted qualitative interpretations of the quantitative LIWC output. Table S.1 lists the word categories we studied to gain insight into the Iran election and describes how we interpreted the attitude or mood expressed.

Table S.1
Word Categories Indicating Public Opinion and Mood and How We Interpreted Them

Word Categories	Attitude or Mood Expressed
First-person singular pronouns	Feelings of depression within the population[a]
Second-person pronouns	An intent and desire to interact with others[b]
Plural pronouns	A sense of (1) group or collective identity and (2) coping with shared trauma[c]
Positive emotions	Feeling generally good or happy (based on LIWC's accuracy in capturing emotions)[d]
Negative emotions	The degree to which people have been affected by a given trauma; also feeling angry, anxious, or sad[e]
Swear/curse words	Frustration or anger

[a] Pennebaker and Chung (2005); Gortner and Pennebaker (2003).

[b] Slatcher, Vazire, and Pennebaker (2008).

[c] Cohn, Mehl, and Pennebaker (2004); Pennebaker, Mehl, and Niederhoffer (2003); Chung and Pennebaker, (2007).

[d] E.g., Alpers et al. (2005); Kahn et al. (2007).

[e] Cohn, Mehl, and Pennebaker (2004).

---

1 Hashtags are words or phrases preceded with the # symbol. Twitter users use hashtags to label their tweets, so tweets with the "IranElection" hashtag are labeled as being about the election.

2 The reason for tweeting in English may have been a strong sense of needing to communicate across national boundaries what was happening in the country.

Placing the LIWC Output into a Politico-Historical Context

In the final phase of our work, we looked for patterns in the data and interpreted those patterns in relation to specific events on the ground and to public figures and topics important during the post-election period. For example, we sought spikes and dips in word usage—i.e., sudden reactions to a specific event or action (e.g., a protest or holiday) that might offer insight into public opinion about that event.[3] We also looked for patterns in comparisons of certain word categories against others.

A Demonstration of LIWC Using Twitter: Insights into Public Mood and Opinion in Iran in the Aftermath of the 2009 Presidential Election

Our work with LIWC enabled us to draw a number of conclusions about the opinion and mood of Twitter users on a wide range of topics during the post-election period. We present a selection here.[4]

As of the end of February 2010, the opposition movement did not appear likely to protest against the government in the foreseeable future. We examined whether increases or decreases in the levels of anger people expressed about the election coincided with—or even forecasted—the outbreak of protests. One word category conveying strong emotion stood out the most clearly: swearing. With each large-scale protest,[5] rates of swearing spiked on Twitter, or rose in the weeks leading up to the event. This suggests that swearing levels could predict the outbreak of protests (see Figure S.1). For example, levels of swearing were elevated in the weeks before the Quds Day protest (September 18, 2009), one of the major protests of the post-election period, and there was a large spike at the end of December, when a protest on Ashura Day occurred. The overall trend in swearing—a gradual decline over time to a relatively stable level lower than the initial level observed in June and July 2009—suggests that the opposition movement had probably resigned itself to the political situation nine months after the election.

President Ahmadinejad initially spurred more anger than Mir Hussein Mousavi, but the opposite had become true by the end of the post-election period. Trends in swearing show that in the initial weeks after the election, people used more profanity when tweeting about Ahmadinejad than about leading opposition candidate Mousavi. However, this pattern had reversed itself by the end of the post-election period, suggesting that when the opposition movement flagged in February 2010, Twitterers felt angrier at Mousavi than Ahmadinejad.

After some early frustration, Twitter users generally viewed President Obama without ill feeling in the aftermath of the election. Our analysis indicates more negative sentiment toward Supreme Leader Khamenei and President Ahmadinejad than toward President Obama throughout the entire post-election period. Indeed, Twitterers displayed little anger toward Obama. One of the few exceptions was early after the election, when they expressed a strong desire for him to take a public stand in support of the Iranian protesters. Linguistic patterns in the tweets also indicated that Twitterers felt a greater sense of community and shared ties

---

[3] Such correlations do not necessarily indicate causal relationships.

[4] An interactive web tool presenting Twitter data from this study is available on RAND's website (RAND National Security Research Division, 2011). Users may select and view combinations of word categories and political topics. The trends displayed show how public opinion and mood changed across time about the topic selected.

[5] By *large-scale*, we mean protests involving hundreds of thousands or millions of people.

Figure S.1
Rates of Swearing on Twitter After the 2009 Presidential Election

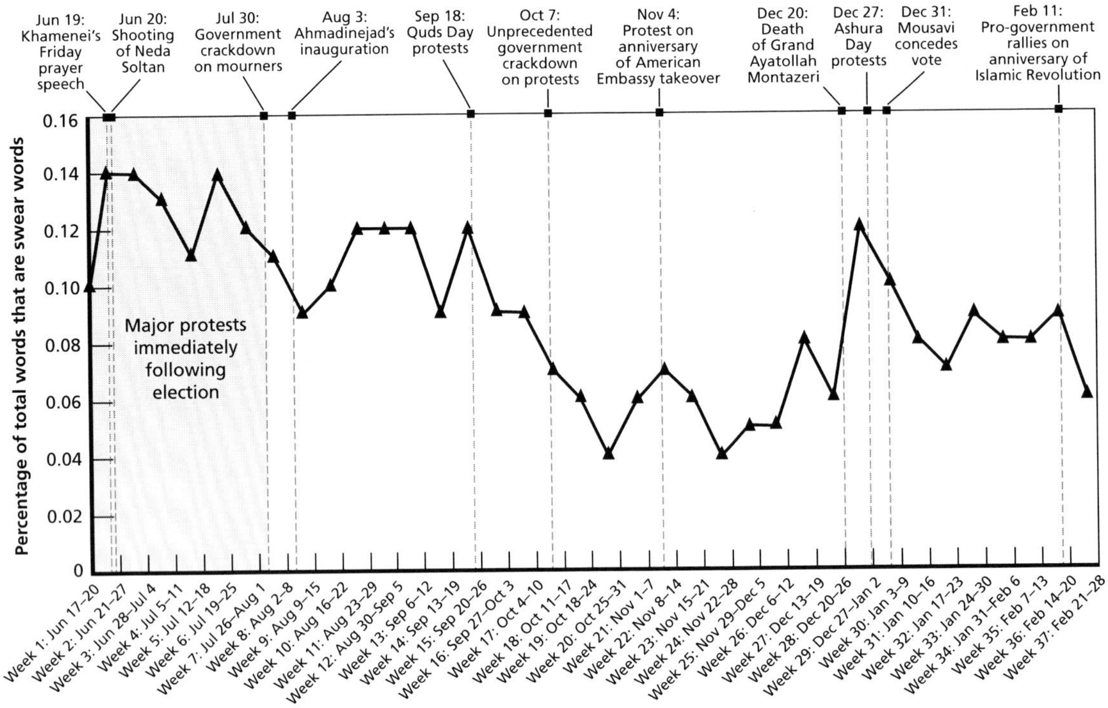

NOTES: The data points signify a ratio of the number of swear words to total words across an entire week's worth of tweets. Significant events in the aftermath of the election are noted at the top of the figure.
RAND *TR1161-S.1*

with each other when discussing Obama than when they discussed Ahmadinejad, Khamenei, Mousavi, or Karroubi.

The Green Movement was viewed more positively than the Islamic Revolutionary Guards Corps and the Basij. The Green Movement is the broad-based opposition movement that developed in the weeks following the presidential election. The Revolutionary Guards are an elite military force and currently Iran's most powerful economic, social, and political institution. The Basij comprises a set of pro-government paramilitary organizations serving under the leadership of the Revolutionary Guards.

In the initial weeks after the election, Twitterers expressed high levels of positive sentiment toward the Green Movement. However, this sentiment dropped sharply after the initial post-election period and remained low until the end of February 2010. With regard to both the Revolutionary Guards and the Basij, Twitterers expressed consistently low levels of positive sentiment throughout the entire period. Between the two, Twitterers expressed more anger at the Basij forces than at the Revolutionary Guards, on the whole.

Countries with traditionally tense relations with Iran were not the target of anger, unlike the "Islamic Republic." Our results suggest that Twitterers did not focus their anger on Iran's traditional enemies—Israel and the United States—in the aftermath of the election. We saw similarly low levels of negative sentiment toward "Iran." But the opposite was true of the "Islamic Republic." This indicates that Twitter users in our sample were angry not at the country of Iran itself but, rather, at the government that rules Iran.

A Methodological Note for Potential Users of the LIWC Software Tool

Our exploratory research raised important considerations for those wishing to use this method. One was especially important. In the current project, the automated analysis provided initial results—suggesting, for example, that tweets containing swear words expressed anger at a certain target. In most cases, the tweets truly did express the emotions signified by the LIWC words they contained. However, in certain cases, tweets that contained words thought to denote sadness, positive emotion, and anxiety did not express the emotion we would have expected, given the words they contained. In that sense, word categories thought to denote a particular set of emotions did not always perform as expected. To manage this problem, analysts could potentially construct alternate, tailored word categories that contain words that seem most useful in context and then validate those categories. Performing this automated analysis therefore alerts the analyst to check specific portions of the data for such anomalies, regardless of whether noteworthy patterns are found.

The Policy Uses of Computer-Based Analysis of Social Media

Our test case of Iran suggests that using the LIWC-based method as a means of analyzing social media holds much promise, particularly in countries where freedom of expression is limited. The potential policy uses are multiple. With this approach, analysts can

- **Make informed assessments of public opinion in countries of interest, in retrospect as well as in real time.** An example is the multiple trends observed among Twitter users that suggested that the opposition movement in Iran had flagged by the end of the nine-month post-election period and would not protest further.
- **Forecast events, such as large-scale protests.** The increase in Twitterers' use of swear words just before large protests formed a suggestive pattern that spikes in swearing could signal an imminent action.
- **Assess the impact of political events or actions on public opinion.** The fact that Twitterers swore at such high levels about Ahmadinejad in the immediate aftermath of the election substantiates the general impression that the election negatively affected public opinion of the Iranian president on a large scale.
- **Inform outreach efforts to foreign populations.** The cursing we saw of President Obama in the earliest weeks after the election, indicating that Twitterers wanted him to take a stand in favor of the opposition, is the type of information that could help the U.S. government, in particular, better understand and act on public opinion in foreign countries.
- **Pinpoint intelligence gaps.** For example, the reversal in public sentiment about President Ahmadinejad and leading opposition candidate Mousavi after the Quds protest raises the question of what drove that change at that time.

Ideas for a Second Phase of This Comprehensive Program of Research

We envision this exploratory work with LIWC as the first phase of a larger program of research. Having now established that LIWC can generate informative output about public mood and opinion in a closed society, we can confidently incorporate it into a multimethod research design to answer timely policy questions, both to validate the method and to explore additional research questions. The upcoming presidential elections in Iran would present one such opportunity. The tightly controlled political climate makes it difficult to obtain direct data on how people inside Iran feel about the candidates and relevant political issues. As such, one could turn to social media to gain needed insights, using LIWC alongside manual analyses of social media posts, interviews of people traveling to and from Iran, and content analyses of articles in the Iranian news media. Similar studies of questions about the Iranian economy or Iran's nuclear weapons program would also be possibilities. Ultimately, we view LIWC and other automated content analysis as an important part of research designs for studies of countries in conflict generally (such as Pakistan or Egypt, as well as Iran)—both to examine them on their own terms and to make comparisons between them.

Acknowledgments

With deep gratitude, we thank Jim Thomson, former president and CEO of RAND, and C. Richard Neu for providing the support needed to conduct this project. We also express our sincere appreciation to Mike Lostumbo for his advice and assistance in formulating a research plan. Mike provided extensive guidance and direction to the project; we gratefully acknowledge his supervision of our efforts. Others at RAND who provided valuable support include Michael Rich and Irv Blickstein. Jack Riley, Eric Peltz, and Jim Dobbins provided extensive feedback during in-progress briefings. John Parachini and Kathi Webb provided additional funding for this work and supported its dissemination to the policy community. Craig Martin and Wally Brechtelsbauer provided technical support. In addition, we thank several people for their direct contributions to this project: Ahmad Rahmani, Wali Shaaker, Francisco Walter, Terry West, and Donna White.

Our three reviewers deserve special recognition for their attention to this report: Jeff Hancock, Julie Taylor, and Craig Charney. Finally, we thank James Pennebaker and Cindy Chung for conducting the groundbreaking research upon which we have built, and for inspiring us to undertake this effort. Their continuing advice and encouragement have been invaluable.

Abbreviations

IP	Internet Protocol
IRGC	Islamic Revolutionary Guard Corps
ISP	Internet service provider
LIWC	Linguistic Inquiry and Word Count
RDS	respondent-driven sampling
SMS	Short Message Service

CHAPTER ONE

Introduction

In 1979, the leader of the Islamic Revolution, Ayatollah Ruhollah Khomeini, garnered vast popular support among the Iranian public by recording his sermons against the Shah onto cassette tapes while he was in exile in France, smuggling them into Iran, and distributing them throughout the country. Although today they may be obsolete, cassette tapes in the 1970s were a relatively new and important innovation in communications technology and played a pivotal role in the lead-up to an event that transformed Iranian history.

More than 30 years after the Islamic Revolution, new Internet-based social media tools, such as blogs, Facebook, Twitter, and YouTube, have replaced cassette tapes as forward-looking communications technologies. And when, in June 2009, Iran faced another history-altering moment—as Iranian state media outlets announced incumbent Mahmoud Ahmadinejad as the winner of a presidential election that millions of Iranians believed to have been fraudulent—these tools decisively influenced the nature of the popular uprising that followed.

June and July 2009 were marked by demonstrations and rallies in the public thoroughfares, squares, and campuses of Iran's cities. Internet-based mobilization was particularly important to these efforts, and the opposition worked quickly and constantly to circumvent restrictions on the Internet imposed by the Iranian regime. Twitter aided initially in bringing protestors into the streets by relaying times and locations of particular demonstrations. But people quickly turned to other social media as well. Entries on individual blogs offered ideas for how to support the Green Movement apart from attending public rallies. Certain bloggers even offered new constitutions for the new Iran they wanted to establish (e.g., Iranian Lawyers for the Green Movement, no date). Facebook pages provided real-time networking and a potential vehicle for disenfranchised Iranians to correspond. As Iranians continued to rally over the months following the election, often in huge numbers, tools such as Twitter and Facebook played an ongoing part in keeping the opposition movement active and connected with domestic and global audiences.

The 2009 Iranian presidential election and its aftermath illustrated the power of social media to help generate political opposition, shape political discourse, and facilitate action in the face of a powerful regime.[1] Iran is a vivid example of the new role social media can now play in authoritarian countries where freedom of expression is limited. Pakistan and China offer similar examples, where citizens who confront restrictions on free speech are using social media to evade government censorship and express opinion publicly (Tavernise, 2010). A par-

[1] The campaigning process and the weeks leading up to the election underlined certain practices and incidents that distinguished this election from those in prior years. The 2009 presidential elections were the most expensive in the history of the Islamic Republic. Election campaigns distributed CDs and DVDs of propaganda and sent tens of millions of text messages with voting information and recommendations. See Peskin, 2009.

ticularly noteworthy example of social media's power as a tool for political organization and communication is that of Egypt, where, in February 2011, widespread protests fueled by online activism eventually forced President Hosni Mubarak to resign.

Analysis of Social Media Can Help Gauge Public Opinion and Mood in Closed Societies

Policymakers and researchers wanting to understand public opinion have used a variety of tools, including surveys (face-to-face or telephone), focus groups, on-site observation, and media analysis. However, in closed societies such as Iran's, where governments censor or punish people for expressing certain views, these options may be limited or unavailable. A recent phone survey of Iranians conducted by the RAND Corporation offers a case in point: While it was possible to conduct such a study, researchers had to avoid asking survey respondents certain questions because of the fearful climate inside Iran (Elson and Nader, 2011).

The relative anonymity of the Internet and social networking sites has given people living in societies with restricted freedom of expression an outlet to express forbidden views. Studying the posts that people in these societies place on social media can help policymakers and researchers gain insight into public opinion on topics that might otherwise have to be avoided. It also provides a way of doing so that is completely unobtrusive to those posting their views.

A New Computer-Based Tool Offers a Promising Means of Tapping into Politically Oriented Content in Social Media

At present, analysts inside the U.S. government are using manual approaches to study social media, which may entail reading a select few blogs and interpreting them. Yet in recent years, automated social media analysis has been increasing, particularly in commercial market research (Macer and Wilson, 2011). In particular, a computer-based analytic tool has been developed that can be used in tandem with the established manual approach to political analysis. Using the two approaches together can address a number of shortcomings involved in using either approach alone.

The automated tool is the Linguistic Inquiry and Word Count (LIWC, pronounced "Luke") 2007 software (Pennebaker, Booth, and Francis, 2007; Pennebaker et al., 2007). This software uses a content analysis method developed for written text—such as text messages posted using social media. The method entails analyzing patterns of word usage thought to reveal psychological states in individuals and groups. LIWC compares the words that appear in a given text against a pre-defined dictionary containing words that have been grouped into linguistic (e.g., pronouns, articles) and psychological (e.g., emotion, cognitive) categories. LIWC then uses these comparisons to calculate ratios indicating the percentage of total words in a text that fall within each category. These ratios represent the relative frequency with which each word category is used in the text. This in turn offers some insight into the writer's emotion, intentions, relationship to his or her audience, etc.

Extensive research has shown certain categories of words to be particularly meaningful. For instance, function words (e.g., pronouns, prepositions, articles)—although they represent a small proportion of overall word use—actually reveal a considerable amount about an individual's psychological state (Chung and Pennebaker, 2007). By performing a qualitative analysis of the quantitative results generated by LIWC—that is, exploring how people's usage of these word categories changes over time and interpreting those changes in a real-life context—one can draw conclusions about public opinion and mood.

Although ample precedent exists for using LIWC in health research, it is largely untested in a political context—particularly with a non-Western population. Our study was designed to take a first step into this new territory. In this report, we will demonstrate how the LIWC-based approach works, the type of output it can generate, and the sort of insights it can lead to, using Iran as a case study. We have analyzed an extensive sample of content from Twitter over the nine months starting with the June 2009 Iranian presidential election and ending in February 2010. We chose to focus on these nine months because the antigovernment protests are understood to have stopped after that time (Nikou, 2010). The goal of our work was to tap into the overall trends in public mood among Twitter users in Iran during what we call the "post-election" period, as well as their opinions on specific political figures and topics.

This Type of Analysis Can Have Important Policy Uses

In addition to breaking new methodological ground, LIWC-based word-usage analysis of social media in the context of such events as the 2009 Iranian presidential election can have important policy uses. We will demonstrate the following uses in this report:

- **Enable Analysts to Assess the Impact of Political Events on Public Opinion.** While surveys provide an explicit measure of public opinion, their results may be biased. Respondents may offer the socially desirable response to certain questions, for example. In closed societies, they may be reluctant to speak freely. In contrast, the implicit patterns of word usage uncovered by LIWC provide an unfiltered perspective, measuring the psychological impact of political events and actions directly.
- **Forecast Important Events in Countries of Interest.** With enough word-usage data from LIWC, it may be possible to build a set of characteristic trends in specific word categories that, when observed, would suggest that a given political event or outcome will occur—protests, for instance, or a large versus small election turnout. Using modeling techniques, analysts could potentially monitor ongoing events in combination with word usage to create forecasts.
- **Inform Outreach Efforts to Foreign Populations.** The United States is beginning to use social media to conduct outreach to foreign populations. The State Department's Digital Outreach Team, for instance, engages people in chat rooms on influential websites in the Muslim world, responding to perceived misinformation and explaining U.S. foreign policy (Bureau of International Information Programs, U.S. Department of State, 2009). The State Department's Opinion Space (U.S. Department of State, no date) is an interactive site that asks users to share their views on U.S. foreign policy (U.S. Department of State, 2010). A better understanding of the mindset and opinions of target populations about various topics—U.S. foreign policy, for example—may increase the effectiveness of such efforts.
- **Help the U.S. Military Understand and Engage People in Its Areas of Operation.** The U.S. military maintains an outreach team that has recently opened communications

with bloggers regarding the U.S. military's role in the global war on terror; for example, contacting bloggers who have posted factually inaccurate material (Alvarez, 2006). But it is unclear to what extent these efforts have been successful in engaging non-U.S. bloggers and blog readers. LIWC-based analysis of content posted on social media in U.S. Central Command's areas of operation may provide insights that can support ongoing outreach and other operations.

- **Pinpoint Intelligence Gaps.** It has been said that there are known unknowns and unknown unknowns.[2] Using LIWC to analyze social media may help address both. When use of a certain word category shifts suddenly, for example, it may suggest that an unknown event of importance has occurred or that a known event is more significant than believed. A gradual change may point to a more general shift in opinion. In this way, intelligence analysts can pinpoint gaps in their understanding of public opinion and mood in countries of interest, helping them plan intelligence collection.

Organization of This Report

In Chapter Two, we describe the LIWC-based methodology we used to analyze our sample of Twitter texts (with additional details provided in the report's appendix). In Chapters Three through Five, we demonstrate that methodology in the context of the 2009 Iranian presidential election, depicting overall trends in mood and then trends in public opinion about Iranian political leaders and organizations, as well as other leaders and countries, such as Israel, the United States, and President Barack Obama. Chapter Six contains methodological considerations that would be of interest to analysts who might want to implement the method. Finally, Chapter Seven presents our vision of the next steps in a comprehensive program of research using the LIWC-based approach.

---

[2] This phrasing was used by former U.S. Secretary of Defense Donald Rumsfeld regarding Iraq, terrorism, and the spread of weapons of mass destruction.

CHAPTER TWO

Methodology

The Precedent for Our Approach: Previous Research Using LIWC and Word-Usage Analysis

Most methods of analyzing verbal communication—text or speech—focus almost exclusively on the subject matter. In contrast, what is unique about the LIWC method of text analysis is that it describes the psychological characteristics of written language (e.g., Alpers et al., 2005) and, potentially, of the writers. In other words, word-usage analysis using LIWC does not rely necessarily on *what* people are explicitly talking or writing about, but *how* they say it implicitly. This allows for conclusions that extend well beyond those that can be drawn from identifying themes in the subject matter and then extracting them. While all word categories can be informative in this regard, *how* people communicate and express themselves largely depends on the function words they use: pronouns, prepositions, articles, conjunctions, and auxiliary verbs (Chung and Pennebaker, 2007). In practical terms, this approach suggests that it is possible to gain insights into emotional states and social disposition, regardless of the content of the writing.

LIWC Has Been Shown to Accurately Represent Verbal Expression

Previous validation work demonstrates that LIWC faithfully represents how people verbally express themselves. First, LIWC accurately captures how people talk and write about their experiences. For instance, a systematic investigation of LIWC's accuracy in measuring emotional expression (Kahn et al., 2007) measured LIWC ratios both in varied emotional writings and in response to emotionally provocative film clips. Kahn and colleagues found that usage of emotion words was, as expected, associated with the emotion (e.g., sad, anxious) expressed in the writings or films, concluding that LIWC represented a "valid method for measuring verbal expression of emotion." Second, the quantitative LIWC results are similar to the qualitative results of text analysis methods commonly used in the social sciences. When the same texts were analyzed, strong correlations were found between word-usage patterns from LIWC and human coders' judgments, suggesting that LIWC analysis closely approximates existing content analysis methods (Alpers et al., 2005).

The Real Potential of Exploring Word Usage Lies in Its Links with Behaviors and Outcomes

LIWC itself simply outputs usage patterns of specific word categories. The real advantage of using this tool lies in a large body of research that links usage of specific word categories with various behaviors and outcomes. For example, an increase in the use of one category of function words, first-person singular pronouns (e.g., "I," "me," my"), is thought to suggest inward or self-focus and is associated with depression (Rude, Gortner, and Pennebaker, 2004). Strikingly, analysis by Stirman and Pennebaker (2001) showed that poets who eventually committed suicide used higher proportions of first-person singular pronouns in their poetry, as compared with poets who did not commit suicide. First-person plural pronouns (e.g., "we," "us," "our"), on the other hand, are thought to indicate attention paid to others or focus on others (Chung and Pennebaker, 2007). Use of these words is associated with better health and tends to increase in times of shared, community-wide turmoil (Cohn, Mehl, and Pennebaker, 2004; Gortner and Pennebaker, 2003; Stone and Pennebaker, 2002). Pronoun use has also been shown to be related to the quality of social interactions. For instance, when communicating in a critical and hostile manner, people may use more first-person singular pronouns (to describe others' negative impact on themselves) and fewer second-person plural pronouns (Simmons, Chambless, and Gordon, 2008).

In other studies, the use of certain emotion words has been linked with physical health. Members of a weight loss blog community who were more successful in losing weight used more sadness words, suggesting that they benefited from sharing strong emotions (Chung et al., 2008). When discussing a traumatic experience, people who used more positive than negative emotion words showed improved physical health (Pennebaker, Mayne, and Francis, 1997).

Word Usage Is Now Being Studied in Politically Oriented Contexts

To date, the associations between word usage and psychological processes have been analyzed primarily in health-related contexts. But recently, researchers have also begun to use LIWC for politically oriented applications, such as terrorism. Pennebaker and Chung (2005) reviewed research on social and psychological responses to terrorism, concluding that "terrorism can have the unintended effects of encouraging affiliation, strengthening values, and reaffirming identities." Pennebaker and Chung's (2008) own examination of al Qaeda transcripts revealed the evolving linguistic styles of Osama bin Laden and Ayman al-Zawahiri. In particular, al-Zawahiri sharply increased his usage of first-person singular pronouns, which, according to Pennebaker and Chung, suggests increased insecurity and feelings of threat over time. LIWC has very recently been used to explore changing emotions in the hours following the 9/11 attacks (Back, Kufner, and Egloff, 2010, 2011). Analyzing an email archive of Enron executives, Keila and Skillicorn (2005) identified linguistic patterns of deception, which Skillicorn and Little (2010) suggest may be applied toward terrorist interrogations or criminal testimony. Hancock and colleagues (2008) found similar patterns of deceptive word use in a study involving text-based conversations. More recently, Hancock and colleagues (2010) outlined a comprehensive approach to identifying linguistic markers of deception and other social and psychological features of communication for terrorists and authoritarian regimes. Finally, LIWC has also been used to compare linguistic styles of the Democratic candidates in the 2000 and 2004 U.S. presidential elections (Pennebaker, Slatcher, and Chung, 2005) and coping with shared trauma over the death of Princess Diana (Stone and Pennebaker, 2002).

Our Research Process

The methodology we used for our LIWC-based word-usage analysis of Twitter in post-election Iran can be divided into three types of tasks. **Planning tasks** began with determining an appropriate sampling plan of social media texts. We also developed sets of (1) relevant political topics and (2) LIWC indicators. Next, **data collection tasks** included constructing the automated program to parse social media texts. Finally, **data analysis tasks** included aggregating data, processing it with LIWC, making comparisons between topics, plotting trend data, and drawing speculative qualitative conclusions. Planning tasks, including our interpretations of LIWC indicators, are discussed below. We discuss data collection and analysis tasks in the appendix.

Planning Tasks: Understanding the Sphere of Relevant Social Media

Selecting Twitter Texts

We used a third-party web tool (TwapperKeeper.com) to download relevant "tweets"—short text messages posted using Twitter—from the time period following the Iran presidential election. Using this archiving tool, individuals were able to create archives to store tweets on specific topics. The topics were self-identified using hashtags, a form of metadata with which to label, or "tag," content as being related to a certain topic.[1] We pulled all the tweets from an existing TwapperKeeper.com archive labeled with the "IranElection" hashtag. At the time of collection (February 2010), this set contained 2,675,679 tweets from June 17, 2009, to February 28, 2010, posted by 124,563 distinct individuals. According to Twitter's official blog, the IranElection hashtag was 2009's second-most popular (and top news-related) topic across all of Twitter (Twitter Blog, 2009b). This archive therefore seemed particularly well suited for this research: Given its overwhelming popularity, the IranElection hashtag appeared to be central to anyone wishing to discuss this topic over Twitter.[2]

Twitter users may label a tweet with any hashtags they choose. For this reason, this method of data collection (i.e., based solely on hashtag) did not distinguish between users living inside and outside of Iran. Although the sample contained users living outside Iran, a review of the tweets themselves suggests that it contained users living inside Iran as well. The following are examples of these tweets:[3]

> Just went to Vanak square site of previous protests. All calm so far
>
> oh my dear god please help us. no one helping us but we still fighting the Basij.
>
> All my friends are coming home Bloody and bones Broken

Other tweets suggest that Twitter users were mobilizing others for protests:

---

[1] Fittingly for social media, hashtags are not an official feature provided by Twitter. Rather, they sprang up organically from the user community as a way to categorize data (Twitter Help Center, no date).

[2] To confirm that IranElection was the key hashtag, we compiled a list of approximately 40 other hashtags related to Iran and to the elections. For several months into data collection, we monitored these hashtags for activity (i.e., popularity) and relevance. This was useful because several of these hashtags were date- or event-driven (e.g., "22Khordad," "22Bahman"). Over this period, none of the other hashtags approached the popularity of the IranElection hashtag. While these less-popular hashtags may have represented different populations, with different attitudes and opinions, our analysis of the most popular hashtag (IranElection) tapped the broadest population available.

[3] The text of the quoted tweets is presented exactly as it appears in the archive.

> Please join Mousavi Khatami and Karoubi tomorrow at 4pm from Enghelab Square to Azadi square in Tehran for a crucial green protest - Mousavi Karoubi and Khatami will attend - (From Iran trusted) thanks

> 5pm SILENT PROTEST 7 Tir Square today wednesday - Anything else is not true TAKE FLOWERS let everyone know retweet others

Finally, we saw possible evidence of Iranians and people in other countries using Twitter to communicate with each other:

> Iranians please post pics of injuries from acid this needs to be verified

These examples suggest that both Iranians as well as people outside Iran—for example, Iranian exiles or non-Iranian supporters of the protest movement—communicated over Twitter using the IranElection hashtag. Consequently, the IranElection archive should contain a broad range of opinion that reflects these interactions. Also of note is that this archive contained only English-language tweets. If people used Twitter to communicate across national boundaries about what happened in Iran, as shown in the examples above, this may help explain why Iranians living inside the country tweeted in the English language rather than in Persian. Finally, using an archive of English-language writings posted over social media suggests that it reflects a population segment that is younger, more educated, and more urban than the overall population of Iran. However, the predominant usage of this hashtag strongly suggests that it encompasses the vast majority of communications regarding the Iran election and subsequent protests and, consequently, that it captures the broadest account of public opinion available.[4]

Selecting Iran-Relevant Political Topics

To explore various aspects of Iranian public opinion, we selected topics of general Iranian political relevance, which included domestic and international affairs. In particular, these topics included leading Iranian political figures (e.g., Ahmadinejad, his election opponents Mir Hussein Mousavi and Mehdi Karroubi), Iranian political institutions and groups (Islamic Revolutionary Guard Corps, Green Movement), as well as the United States and President Obama.

Selecting the LIWC Word Categories to Use in Our Analysis and Defining How We Would Interpret Them

Research linking use of specific words to psychological states and behaviors formed the basis of the indicators we chose to look at. We relied on precedents from this literature to develop a system for interpreting social media use after the Iranian presidential election. We concentrated on linguistic function categories (e.g., pronouns) and on word categories indicating strongly expressed opinions and mood.

First-Person Singular Pronouns. Usage of first-person singular pronouns (e.g., "I," "me," "my") reflects a self-focus that may have several possible interpretations. For instance, self-focus may suggest depression; people who are depressed use more "I" pronouns in their language (Rude, Gortner, and Pennebaker, 2004). After large-scale tragedies, usage of these pronouns

---

[4] Chapter Three discusses in further detail social media use in Iran during this time.

has been shown to signify depressive states, low self-esteem, and low dominance (Pennebaker and Chung, 2005). Following such traumatic events, elevated usage of first-person singular pronouns that takes place over extended periods of time and is directed to large groups or audiences may indicate excessive self-focus that reflects poor coping with that tragedy and depression (Cindy K. Chung, personal communication, June 2011). We therefore propose that the self-focus implied by this word category may serve as a general indicator of depression or negative emotional states in the population.

For those who protested it, the Iranian election arguably constituted a traumatic event, suggesting that use of first-person singular pronouns after the election might follow similar patterns and have a similar meaning as after other relevant traumatic events. Thus, given usage trends following certain social upheavals and traumatic events, we interpreted usage of these words after the Iranian election as a measure of depression among the population.[5] For example, after the collapse of thousands of logs onto students at Texas A&M University, the university newspaper covered the traumatic event for several months. In studying the language used in this coverage, Gortner and Pennebaker (2003) found that use of first-person singular pronouns peaked in the week after the tragedy before gradually decreasing over the next eight weeks. The writings surrounding this tragedy resembled those during the Iran protests in two important ways (Cindy K. Chung, personal communication, June 2011). First, for both the Texas A&M students and Iranian protesters, the respective traumatic events were physically proximal and personally emotional. Second, writings on both these tragedies appear to be intended for a fairly proximal audience: The student newspaper articles were intended to be read by Texas A&M students, and many people who sent tweets about the Iran election directly addressed a large number of other interested parties (e.g., protesters, as well as people who wished to help).

Following the 9/11 attacks, however, bloggers writing in the immediate aftermath of the tragedy decreased their usage of the "I" pronoun for three days immediately after the attacks. In addition, they continued to use the "I" pronoun at lower rates for the next two months after the attacks, through early November (Cohn, Mehl, and Pennebaker, 2004). This pattern, reversed from that which was observed for the Texas A&M tragedy, also differs in that the bloggers' writings were more likely for a larger, more distant audience with whom there was likely minimal interaction. In the Cohn, Mehl, and Pennebaker study, the usage of first-person singular pronouns combined with other indicators was interpreted as people attempting to psychologically distance themselves from the event—that is, thinking about it as more remote and separate from themselves.

For the Iran protests, a psychological-distancing interpretation for usage of first-person singular pronouns seems less appropriate as compared with the depression interpretation. This is because the protests and demonstrations were clearly visible and visceral to those who actually participated in them. Furthermore, people attempting to organize information and coordinate protests—whether inside or outside Iran—would seem to be highly invested psychologically in the traumatic events, rather than attempting to distance themselves from those events.

Second-Person Pronouns. We interpreted usage of second-person pronouns (e.g., "you," "yours")—both singular and plural—as signaling intent and desire to interact with others. Generally speaking, these pronouns may indicate focus or attention paid to others (Slatcher,

---

[5] Here we mean *depression* not in the sense of a clinical disorder, but more in the sense of depressed mood.

Vazire, and Pennebaker, 2008). In particular, usage of these pronouns may have a slightly negative quality. Previous research has (only weakly) associated their use with more critical and hostile interactions and with lower relationship satisfaction and quality (Simmons, Chambless, and Gordon, 2008).

Plural Pronouns. Usage of plural pronouns—that is, references to multiple people (e.g., "we," "us")—were taken as indicators of (1) group or collective identity and (2) coping with shared trauma. In the wake of a trauma, people can also be expected to focus more intensely on their relationships with others—seeking and sharing social support, or increasing a sense of collective identity or community. Linguistically, people signal their increased concern with social dynamics after a traumatic event by making more frequent references to other people, such as by using more second-person, third-person, and first-person plural pronouns (Pennebaker, Mehl, and Niederhoffer, 2003). Previous research concerning the use of third-person pronouns (e.g. "she," "he," "they") also suggests that people use these when coping and adapting after a traumatic event (Chung and Pennebaker, 2007).

Positive Emotions. We used positive-emotion words as a sort of "approval rating." Previous research has demonstrated that emotional word usage is accurately represented in LIWC (e.g., Alpers et al., 2005; Kahn et al., 2007). Our broad interpretation of expressions of positive emotion was therefore straightforward—usage of positive-emotion words indicated that people were generally feeling good or happy.[6] In analyses of specific political events or figures, we interpreted this indicator as approval of that event or figure.

Negative Emotions. How people cope with shared trauma is a major theme of this research. Lingering negative emotions after an upheaval indicate the degree to which people have been affected, and thus lingering negative emotions may be a useful indirect measure of whether or how negatively people viewed the elections (Cohn, Mehl, and Pennebaker, 2004). Separately, expressions of various negative emotions—anger, anxiety, and sadness—each constituted an important, unique indicator of public mood.

Swear/Curse Words. The most common usage of curse words is likely to express frustration or anger, although people may also swear when excited or surprised. Generally, people tend to be extremely emotional when using swear words. In this research, we used the simplest and most likely interpretation, that usage of swear words indicated frustration and anger.

---

6 We explored only one indicator for positive emotions, tracking negative emotions (i.e., anger, anxiety, and sadness) separately. Positive emotions, such as joy or amusement, are relatively difficult to distinguish from one another, while negative emotions, such as anger or sadness, are fairly distinct (Fredrickson, 2003).

CHAPTER THREE

Background on Social Media Use in Iran and Events Surrounding the 2009 Election

Social Media Use in Contemporary Iran

In the Islamic Republic of Iran, social media has become a powerful political tool. Never was this more apparent than during the country's 2009 presidential election and its aftermath. Following a contentious outcome that returned the far-right conservative Mahmoud Ahmadinejad to office for a second term, social media was used heavily by both sides of a starkly divided political spectrum—at first, by the opposition Green Movement and millions of Iranians who contested Ahmadinejad's reelection, and then increasingly by the conservative government and other supporters of the official results. Whether to spread information, organize demonstrations, conduct surveillance, or sway public opinion, social media was used in a variety of ways that drove political developments and shaped Iran's political landscape.

The intensive use of social media for political purposes during this period stemmed from an already widespread base of Internet users in Iran, the anonymity that tools such as Twitter and blogs offered, and the well-established popularity of these interactive services. While this trend peaked with the 2009 elections, it had begun in Iran well before that and continues today.

The Scale of Internet and Social Media Usage in Contemporary Iran

In contemporary Iran, literacy is high and Internet use common. In 2008, out of a population of roughly 72 million, there were almost 23 million Internet users in Iran (taking private and public users[1] together)—in other words, about 32 Internet users for every 100 people; by 2009, Internet users had increased to 27.9 million—34 percent of the population (World Bank Group, 2010).[2] Use of mobile phones is also widespread. As of 2009, Iran had 30.2 million mobile phone users (Freedom House, 2009), with 72 cellular subscriptions for every 100 people (World Bank, no date).

The Iranian Internet market is divided into a single public Internet service provider (ISP) and more than 50 private ISPs. The public ISP dominates the market, with the private providers dependent on the regime-run Iranian Telecommunications Company (Reports Without Borders, 2009). These private ISPs must officially register with the regime and deploy the same regime-approved filtering system that the public ISP is required to use.

---

1 Public users include individuals who use the Internet on a public computer in Internet cafés, for example.

2 Statistics on Internet penetration in Iran, however, are disputed, and significantly lower numbers have been reported, e.g., Freedom House, 2011.

Persian is one of the most widely used languages on the Internet and, specifically, in the blogosphere (BBC News, "Blogosphere Sees Healthy Growth," November 8, 2006). A diverse assortment of personal and collective Persian-language blogs cuts across the Iranian ideological spectrum. According to BBC reports, Persian first entered the top ten languages of the blogosphere in 2006.[3] Today while Iran has the 19th-largest population in the world, its blogosphere holds the third spot in terms of number of users, just behind the United States and China.

Twitter, Facebook, and text messaging are highly popular modes of correspondence and networking in Iran as well. On Twitter, tweets posted in Iran[4] are typically either in Persian; in Persian transliterated into English; or in some alternative language, most often English.[5] As it is impossible to determine how many Iranians use Twitter, it is impossible to quantify how many of them are writing in Persian, as opposed to English or other languages.

Who Is Using Social Media in Iran?

Social media in Iran are used by a broad cross-section of society that includes the young, students, intelligentsia, and, recently, supporters of the Green Movement. Supporters of the current right-wing government, conservative and religious Iranians, and even the security forces also use social media to disseminate ideas, mobilize support, and, in the case of the government, maintain the status quo (Tehrani, 2009). Though the exact identities or characteristics of Iran's social media users cannot be determined, a 2008 social network analysis of the Persian blogosphere suggests a broad diversity of political ideology, social conservatism, age, and gender (Kelly and Etling, 2008).

The Anonymity Factor

Facebook, Twitter, and popular blog hosts such as Wordpress and Blogspot cannot definitively ascertain users' true identities. Though Facebook often prevents new users from establishing profiles under clearly fictitious names,[6] pseudonyms are allowed and new users are not required to enter personal data. Twitter accepts all usernames and requires no personal data. It has developed a "geo-tagging" tool to attempt to identify users by geographical location, although this tool may be manipulated. Blogs, like Twitter, also require no entry of personal data.

In short, Facebook, Twitter, and blog users can control what is revealed and what is kept private on their social media profiles. People may abbreviate their names, operating as John D., for example, instead of John Doe. Alternatively, they may create pseudonyms for themselves, like Green Martyr or Truth Defender. Because of this, Internet-based social media create challenges for governments such as Iran's that might arrest users for posting prohibited content.

---

[3] According to the 2006 BBC report (BBC News, "Blogosphere Sees Healthy Growth," November 8, 2006), English, Japanese, and Chinese held the first three spots. Kornacki (2006), however, suggests that Persian was the second most popular language in the entire blogosphere in 2006.

[4] Note that because of issues of attribution, it is not possible to verify that these individuals are in Iran, or necessarily Iranian.

[5] As there are considerable populations of the Iranian diaspora in the United States, Canada, and Europe, Iranians inside Iran may often choose to correspond in European languages so as to develop ties with the diaspora.

[6] Facebook does not allow profiles under names that are not personal (although organizations and movements may establish Fan Pages for themselves). So, although establishing a new Facebook profile under a name like "Iran Activist" is not necessarily possible under current Facebook limitations, using an altered personal name is possible. This affords Iranians and those operating in similar environments the opportunity to use Facebook under a pseudonym or modified version of their real name.

The ability to use social media without providing personal data makes it less likely that individuals behind politically perilous posts will be identified. Indeed, by using pseudonyms and anonymous email addresses to set up their profiles, Iranian social media users could post political content after the 2009 election with reduced potential for consequences from the government. Blogs, for example, were attributed to such names as Bachayeh Ghalam, or "Child of the Pen," and Jama'at-e Javanan-e Sabz-e Iran, or "Group of Green Youth of Iran."

The relatively modest equipment needed to use social media provides an additional layer of anonymity. Whereas print media requires physical distribution, Facebook, Twitter, blogs, and text messages can be accessed through portable hand-held devices. Twitter requires no more than a basic mobile telephone, because the 140-character tweets can be posted as simple text messages. Posting to social media sites from a public computer also complicates efforts to identify users. Many Iranian Internet users who do not own computers may do so inadvertently by using public computers.

The Iranian Information Environment Prior to the 2009 Presidential Election

Iran's information environment blossomed under the presidency of Mohammad Khatami (1997–2005), whose government significantly relaxed censorship and allowed hundreds of reformist newspapers and journals to operate in relative freedom. It was during this period that the Internet first became an important means of communication in Iran and Iranians began using social media in earnest: Several newspapers and journals developed online presences, and Persian language blogs proliferated. Some of these blogs were devoted to news and political discussion; many others provided an outlet for the individual viewpoints and experiences of thousands of Iranians.

However, when Mahmoud Ahmadinejad first came to power in August 2005, he reversed Mohammad Khatami's liberalization of most media. Under his leadership, the Iranian government took tight control of radio, television, and print outlets. The Islamic Republic Broadcast Corporation operated all television and radio channels in the country. In addition, all non governmental print media were subjected to government censorship: Those deemed to violate government rules and standards were regularly shut down. Iran's Supreme National Security Council began to issue regular guidelines to newspapers regarding "red lines" in reporting; for example, stories on the nuclear program.

Ahmadinejad's government also took decisive steps to curb use of the Internet in Iran. To a large degree, it was successful. By 2009, the regime had cut off access to millions of websites (Rhoads and Chao, 2009). In March 2009, Reporters Without Borders placed Iran among the world's 12 top countries known for effectively censoring news and information and systematically repressing Internet users (Reports Without Borders, 2009). One month later, in April 2009, just before the presidential election, the Majles (Parliament) passed a bill that required all candidates to register their blogs and Internet sites with the Ministry of Culture and Islamic Guidance.[7]

Facebook was a particular target of censorship during Ahmadinejad's first term in office. In 2006, his administration cut off access to Facebook and made its use illegal. In February 2009, the government legalized its use, but this was short-lived: Facebook was prohibited once more on May 23, 2009, just before the presidential election scheduled for June 12 (Cashmore,

---

[7] Government restrictions on the Internet extended beyond Tehran, as users in Qom, Ahvaz, Karaj, Tabriz, Boushehr, Mashhad, and Shiraz were all subject to the same controls and monitoring.

2009). Yet just three days later, on May 26, the regime reversed position and again lifted restrictions on its use.

Opinions vary as to why the government, in the five months before the election, vacillated about Facebook. According to some, by allowing Iranians the freedom to use Facebook, the regime hoped to bolster its image as legitimate and progressive, giving the impression that Iranian citizens would be permitted more freedom than in the past—something particularly important in the months before a presidential election. Another view suggests that, by restoring legal access to Facebook, the regime provided itself the ideal opportunity to monitor those who felt free enough to express themselves on the Internet, and arrest them when it saw fit. A third view holds that the regime may have loosened restrictions surrounding Facebook for its own benefit, as conservatives and religious figures in the Iranian Shi'ite hierarchy also used social media to propagate their own ideology.

The Use of Social Media During the 2009 Presidential Election in Iran

On June 12, 2009, Islamic Republic–controlled media announced a surprise landslide reelection victory for Ahmadinejad only hours after the polls closed. Thousands of Iranians took to the streets to stage mass protests, chanting, "Where is my vote?" Perhaps anticipating the role that effective communication and networking could play in organizing demonstrations, the government had cut off mobile phone and text messaging services before the polls opened that morning (Jardin, 2009). Service reportedly remained unavailable the day after the election, June 13 (BBC News, 2009d). But this measure did not quash Mousavi's supporters or stamp out the protests, which expanded in number and strength well beyond Tehran into more traditionally conservative regions of the country. Iran's Supreme Leader Ayatollah Ali Khamenei, who gave Ahmadinejad decisive support right after the election, became a particular target of the demonstrators' anger—decades of chanting "Death to America, Death to Israel" were suddenly replaced by "Death to the Dictator."

The Green Movement (Jonbesh e Sabz) was born directly of this opposition to Ahmadinejad's reelection. The two reformist presidential candidates, former Prime Minister Mir Hussein Mousavi and former Parliament Speaker Mehdi Karroubi, emerged as its leaders. The Green Movement relied heavily on Twitter, Facebook, text messaging, and the thousands of blogs created by ordinary Iranians to quickly organize and coordinate opposition efforts and public demonstrations, as well as to disseminate doctrine and political manifestos.[8] These social media tools played a pivotal role in the drive to circumvent government censorship and secure broad support from different, often conflicting, strata within the Iranian populace.

The global nature of social media and the inability of observers to distinguish Iran-based users from users elsewhere helped the Green Movement considerably. With Twitter, for example, in the days immediately following the election, appeals spread throughout the world: "Change your location on Twitter to Tehran, Iran." "Change your time settings to GMT + 3:30." By multiplying the number of Twitter users who appeared to be in Iran, these appeals helped protect those Iranian users who actually were in the country by making it far more difficult for state operatives to seek out and detain individuals tweeting against the establishment. The ability provided by social media to remain in touch with the Iranian diaspora and

---

8 Such manifestos were not necessarily endorsed or accepted by the entire Green Movement. The Green Movement has been a very broad and fractious population of people, and different individuals or sets of individuals affiliated with it held different views of what should constitute its doctrine, the new constitution of the new Iranian Republic, etc.

the rest of the world became especially important once the regime banned foreign journalists from covering the presidential election—and, in some cases, jailed them (Athanasiadis, 2009).

Twitter itself helped Iranians use the tool for political purposes during this critical time. The company had scheduled maintenance that would render the service unavailable on June 16, 2009, between 9:15 and 10:45 a.m. in Tehran. Right after the election, users created a viral campaign to pressure Twitter to reschedule the work. Using hashtags such as #NoMaintenance and #TwitterStayUp, the campaign called for Twitter to perform the maintenance at 4:00 a.m. Tehran time instead, to allow the streams of correspondence between Iran-based Twitter users to continue uninterrupted. By 5:00 p.m. on June 15, 2009, Twitter announced that it would change its upgrade time to 2:00–3:00 p.m. Pacific Standard Time on June 16, 2009—1:30 a.m. in Tehran (Twitter Blog, 2009a; Stelter and Stone, 2009a).

Facebook also took quick steps as a result of the uprisings. A mere six days after the presidential election, the company released a beta version of its entire site in Persian (Kwan, 2009). In a posting on Facebook's blog, a Facebook engineer reported that the company had created the Persian version to accommodate the volume of news and information shared on Facebook in Persian. With the help of more than 400 Persian speakers, Facebook rapidly made the site much easier for Iranians to navigate and use (Parr, 2009b).

YouTube also played a part by loosening its usual prohibitions against graphically violent videos (Stelter and Stone, 2009a). As a result, videos of the Iranian upheaval were broadcast extensively on YouTube, capturing the attention of its massive, international user base. According to a June 17, 2009, report from the website *Mashable*,[9] 3,000 Iran-related videos were uploaded to YouTube within a 24-hour period (Parr, 2009a). The large volume of footage from inside Iran gave international viewers a window into the opposition movement during this critical time.

The Role of Social Media in Iran's Internal Politics Grew Rapidly After the 2009 Presidential Election

In the weeks and then months after the election, the Iranian information environment became progressively more repressive. The Iranian government cut Internet traffic within Iran drastically in the early post-election weeks, for example (Stelter and Stone, 2009a). The website of a program, produced by the Islamic Revolutionary Guards Corps (IRGC), on state television called *Gerdab*—a show originally aimed at exposing the "immorality" of bloggers—started posting photographs of Iranian protestors and requesting that visitors to the site identify them. Reports emerged in late June 2009 that the Iranian regime was intentionally permitting Internet traffic to and from social networking sites such as Facebook and Twitter so that it could use a sophisticated practice called deep packet inspection to collect information about users (Tompkins, 2009; Rhoads and Chao, 2009). It was reportedly also applying the same technology to monitor mobile phone communications (Cellan-Jones, 2009).

It therefore became critical for members of the opposition to find a means of communication that offered relative freedom against retribution from the regime. Social media met this need. Despite the reports of monitoring, Iranians who supported the Green Movement used Facebook, blogs, and Twitter to disseminate political propaganda, decry political actions, condemn public figures, and organize demonstrations. These tools decentralized the power to effect change and the responsibility to act, enabling any individuals in the Green Movement

[9] *Mashable* is a heavily trafficked news site and Internet news blog focused on social media news.

to communicate their messages and needs, even when top leaders were either directly restricted or too intimidated to do so themselves. For instance, in June and July 2009, supporters of the Green Movement in and outside of Iran initiated multiple Internet-based campaigns to take down the *Gerdab* website (Cyberwar4iran, 2009; *Gerdab*, 2009). On one website, NedaSites, a supporter of the Green Movement, even pleaded openly with *Gerdab*'s programmers and employees to reconsider their willingness to help identify protestors (Great Iran, 2009).

During this time, public figures from Iran's political and religious establishments communicated through social media without the use of pseudonyms. Leaders affiliated with the Green Movement engaged in social media publicly as well, maintaining personal blogs despite intimidation and threats of physical violence. But most Iranians in the opposition attempted to remain anonymous, commonly through the use of computer proxy servers.[10] As the regime increasingly banned access to the most popular proxies in the early post-election period, members of the Green Movement began using social media to trade lists of other open proxies (Stelter and Stone, 2009b). Monitoring these announcements, the regime would then immediately blacklist these proxies. But supporters of the Green Movement outside of Iran continued to set up new proxy servers that offered users inside Iran the ability to access the Internet with periodically changing Internet Protocol (IP) addresses. These proxy servers were effectively "digital safe houses that [could] strip out identifying information and allow Iranians to view blocked Web sites" (Stelter and Stone, 2009b). Another option was volunteer-run services like the Tor Project that masked Internet traffic by bouncing Internet connections between separate computers. Tor reported a tenfold increase in traffic from Iran in the week after the election (Stelter and Stone, 2009b).

Twitter was particularly important during this tumultuous period because it was less vulnerable to the regime's restrictions on and monitoring of the Internet. In contrast to blogs and Facebook, use of Twitter was distinctly difficult to extinguish because the technology has several points of access and does not require individuals to have Internet access in order to post tweets (Segan, 2009). Cost played an important role: Whereas hand-held devices with Internet access could be cost-prohibitive for many Iranians, basic mobile phones were inexpensive and a standard item for the urban Iranian population.[11] People could easily and cheaply use their phones to post tweets via text messages. Iranians and those tweeting about Iran became so prevalent on Twitter that, on Twitter's "Top Twitter Trends of 2009," three of the ten trends in the "News Events" category were related to Iran, with the "IranElection" hashtag in first place, the "Iran" hashtag at fourth, and the "Tehran" hashtag at fifth.

As members of the opposition looked for ways to evade government retribution, the regime expanded its efforts. The IRGC's Center for Investigating Organized Cyber Crimes took on a heightened role, for example. Originally founded in 2007 partly "to investigate and confront social and economic offenses on the internet" (Foreign Affairs Committee of the National Council of Resistance of Iran, 2010), the center became increasingly important over the course of 2009 as the regime combated the opposition's online activities.

The Ahmadinejad government also began to co-opt for its own benefit the very social networking tools the opposition had used against it. In the late autumn of 2009, it started sending intimidating and threatening text messages to protesters and would-be protestors. These

[10] A proxy is a computer system that acts as a gateway between a sender and receiver of Internet information. One of its potential purposes is to keep machines behind the proxy anonymous.

[11] As of 2009, Iran had 30.2 million mobile phone users (Freedom House, 2009).

messages would warn the recipients against, for example, attending protests (Masnick, 2010; World Bank Group, 2010). Government security forces also threatened Facebook and blog users. Reports alleged that by December 2009 the government had extended these measures to Iranians living abroad in the form of threats and intimidating correspondence targeting Iranian émigrés who had spoken against the Iranian regime (Fassihi, 2009).

At the same time, websites continued to be filtered and Internet traffic blocked. In one high-profile example, the opposition had scheduled large demonstrations for February 12, 2010, to coincide with the anniversary of the Islamic Revolution. Leading up to the event, the Islamic Republic again suspended access to Google's Gmail. Reports also circulated of widespread interruptions to Internet service and text messaging (Warren, 2010; Jardin, 2009; Rhoads, Cummins, and Vascellaro, 2010).

By dominating traditional media and infiltrating the same social media it had systematically repressed, the Iranian establishment under President Ahmadinejad succeeded in consolidating considerable power over the information environment in the nine months following the presidential election (Amos, 2010). At the same time, the Green Movement gradually lost momentum. Although it sustained popular opposition to the election results from June 2009 until February 2010, after that time, its broad, fractious nature proved to be a liability and its leaders came under increasing pressure from the regime. As this happened, Iranians in the opposition began to use social media for different purposes. Twitter and Facebook no longer served solely to unify and coordinate. Instead, Iranians began to increasingly use these tools to express dissatisfaction with both the Green Movement and international leadership for their perceived failure to meaningfully change the fate of the Iranian people.

Yet the now-subdued Green Movement still relied heavily on the Internet and social media to communicate a multipronged message regarding the authoritarian nature of the Iranian regime and the importance of reform and to show that the movement was still alive despite the lack of overt protests. One year after the election, Mousavi's website, Kalemeh.com, though operated from abroad, remained a key channel of communication for the opposition leader (Amos, 2010; Erdbrink, 2010).

Major Events in Iran During the Post-Election Period

The contested presidential election in June 2009 triggered a spate of events over the next nine months in which the broad-based opposition movement posed a highly visible challenge to the government of the Islamic Republic. Many of these events were unpredictable. But certain events on the Persian and historical Iranian calendars generated more predictable surges in demonstrations. These events provide the backdrop against which we examined public opinion and mood among Twitterers in the post-election period.

The Rise of Mass Protests

The largest street demonstrations (with protestors numbering in the hundreds of thousands, or even millions) took place beginning immediately after the election through the month of July 2009. On June 13, the day the election results were announced, more than 100 reformists were arrested.[12] Protests took place at Tehran University, Amirkabir University, and Shahid Beheshti University, and large demonstrations arose in cities across the country. Within 48 hours, the regime raided dormitories at Sharif University, and 120 members of the faculty resigned in protest against the election results. On June 15, the regime raided Shiraz University as well. By June 16, 120 lecturers at the University of Tehran had also resigned in protest. Mousavi called for a day of mourning on June 18, and massive mourning rallies—reminiscent of those held in 1979 during the Islamic Revolution—took place as Iranians honored dead countrymen as martyrs.

June 19: Khamenei's Friday Prayer Speech

On June 19, 2009, in his first public appearance since the presidential election, Ayatollah Khamenei gave a much-anticipated sermon as he led Friday prayers at Tehran University (Helft, 2009). Khamenei took a hard line against the opposition movement, asserting forcefully that the election had been democratic and free and that Ahmadinejad was the victor (Niteowl, 2009). He underlined the threat of severe retaliation against those who continued to demonstrate.

The number of people who gather at the *Khotbeh*, or Friday sermon, may be viewed as a proxy for measuring support for the government. Reports suggest that the regime made a concerted effort to transport Iranians from pro-regime populations, such as in Qom, to the Friday sermon in Tehran to overshadow potential expressions of opposition by the Green Movement (NBC News, 2010). From the opposition, Karroubi and Mousavi both encouraged their supporters not to attend the traditional Friday services. Khamenei's Friday prayer speech was viewed as a consequential blow to the progress and prospects of the Green Movement. After this, the Supreme Leader also became the target of opposition protests.

June 20: Neda Agha-Soltan's Death

On June 20, 2009, a young woman named Neda Agha-Soltan was shot in the chest by a member of the Basij militia during a protest march and died on a Tehran street amid a crowd of demonstrators. Her death was captured on amateur video taken on mobile phones. These videos quickly spread across the world, and soon Neda Agha-Soltan became the iconic face of the Iranian struggle. The hashtag "Neda" became a "trending topic"[13] on Twitter by the end of that day. When the regime prohibited Neda Agha-Soltan's family from holding a public funeral, Karroubi used a Facebook posting to call for public mourning of the young woman (Karroubi, 2009).

July 9: Anniversary of the 1999 Student Uprisings

July 9, 2009, marked the tenth anniversary of the 1999 Iranian student uprisings. Despite restrictions put in place by the regime and the threat from security forces, thousands of Iranians took to the streets to commemorate the uprisings and again protest the election results.

---

[12] Among those arrested was Mohammad Reza Khatami, former Deputy Speaker of the Majles and brother of former President Mohammad Khatami.

[13] Driven by Twitter users, the designation of *trending topic* refers to a word, phrase, or topic that is posted exceptionally widely on Twitter because of concerted effort by users or because of a certain event or incident that prompts people to discuss it. The *trending topic* designation suggests that the topic—be it a person, place, or thing—is a particularly notable topic at that moment.

The demonstration was the first major public gathering after 11 days of relative calm in Tehran (Esfandiari, 2009).

A few days later, on July 13, Grand Ayatollah Hossein Ali Montazeri, the most senior clerical leader and one of the top two *Marja-e Taghlid* (Source of Emulation) in Shi'ite Islam, issued a series of *fatwas*. He called the Supreme Leader illegitimate and asserted that Khamenei had worked with the government to act against religion. Montazeri called on Iranians to take action against injustice in spite of the potential consequences. "Montazeri" began to spread as a hashtag on Twitter (Sahimi, 2009).

However, despite Montazeri's call to action, by the end of July, the government had largely halted the protests (BBC News, 2009a; Worth and Fathi, 2009a; Worth, Fathi, and Zeleny, 2009). Still, the opposition's leaders continued their criticism of the election and the government's violent crackdown.

August 5: Ahmadinejad's Inauguration

On August 5, 2009, the Guardian Council inaugurated Mahmoud Ahmadinejad for a second term as President of the Islamic Republic. Just days earlier, there had been significant upheaval in the government: On July 27, Culture Minister Mohammad Hossein Saffar Harandi resigned and Ahmadinejad fired his Intelligence Minister Gholam-Hossein Mohseni-Ehi. The inauguration also came four days after the regime opened a mass trial against more than 100 opposition protestors for allegedly conspiring with foreign powers to bring down the government.[14]

September 18: Quds Day

After the end to protests in August and the first half of September, large-scale demonstrations resumed on Quds Day, September 18. Tens of thousands of protestors marched through Tehran and other Iranian cities, hijacking a government-sponsored anti-Israel march and injecting new life into the opposition movement (Worth, Fathi, and Zeleny, 2009).

Ayatollah Khomeini introduced Quds Day, the last Friday of Ramadan, as a day to express solidarity with the Palestinian people and oppose Zionism and Israel's control of Jerusalem. In 2009, Iran's chief of police issued a strongly worded warning to the opposition about the consequences of "derailing" Quds Day. Moreover, the regime banned former president Ayatollah Akbar Hashemi Rafsanjani, who had demonstrated support for the Green Movement, from leading the Friday Prayers on Quds Day, although this had traditionally been his responsibility. He was replaced by the hard-line clerical figure Ahmad Khatami, while President Ahmadinejad served as key speaker before the prayers.

The opposition dismissed the stern forewarnings. The 2009 Quds Day protests were particularly momentous because the three opposition leaders—Mousavi, Karroubi, and Mohammad Khatami—joined the crowds in Tehran for the first time in several months (Worth, 2009a), drawing heightened attention to their cause as they accused the regime of torturing and raping imprisoned protestors.

The Quds Day protests were among the last of the truly large-scale opposition protests after the election (Worth, Fathi, and Zeleny, 2009; Fathi, 2009a; Worth, 2009b; Worth and Fathi, 2009b, 2009c). In their aftermath, the government took steps to intensify pressure on the opposition movement and stamp out the demonstrations (Slackman, 2009b). It issued the

---

[14] Of note, Ayatollah Khomeini's grandson, whom the regime expected to attend the inauguration, left Iran and did not attend.

first death sentences to protesters (Slackman, 2009b), appointed two hard-line military veterans to security-related positions (Fathi, 2009b), and shut down pro-reform newspapers (Fathi, 2009b).

Although smaller protests took place at Iran's universities every week until late September, there were no major street demonstrations. A larger protest took place on the anniversary of the takeover of the U.S. embassy (November 4), but it numbered only in the thousands (BBC News, 2009e). Another protest took place on university campuses for National Student Day (December 7), but this too only drew thousands of people rather than the tens of thousands who had rallied on Quds Day (Worth and Fathi, 2009b).

Late December: Ashura Day Protests

The final set of large-scale opposition protests occurred in the days leading up to and on the day of Ashura (December 27), a holiday that serves as a sacred day of mourning for the martyrdom of Imam Hossein, the grandson of the Islamic Prophet Muhammad. In the Islamic calendar, Ashura falls on the tenth day of the sacred month of Muharram, a month of religious observance and mourning. Shi'ite Muslims use this day to replicate the sufferings of Hossein through mass public demonstrations of mourning and self-flagellation.

One week before Ashura Day, on December 20, 2009, Grand Ayatollah Montazeri, the dissident cleric who had become the religious leader of the Green Movement, died. The passing of their religious mentor seemed to reinvigorate the opposition. In the days after his death—including at his funeral on December 21 in the city of Qom—protestors trying to mourn him clashed with police (Fathi, 2009c). The religiously significant seventh day after Montazeri's death happened to fall exactly on Ashura. The rallies held that day were the largest, and also the bloodiest, since those held right after the election (BBC News, 2009f; Worth and Fathi, 2009c).[15] Tens of thousands of opposition protestors took to the streets, resulting in several violent confrontations. The regime's security forces opened fire on the protestors, with Ali Habibi-Mousavi, Mousavi's nephew, among those killed. Karroubi and Mousavi declared December 28 a national day of mourning and invited Iranians to Qom, the place of Montazeri's death.

February 11, 2010: 31st Anniversary of the Islamic Revolution

A few days after the Ashura protests, Mousavi offered a prescription for solving the political crisis that did not involve holding a new vote (BBC News, 2010a; Slackman, 2010a). Almost a month later, Karroubi and former president Khatami followed suit by dropping their demand for a new presidential election, saying that although they still believed the vote in June was fraudulent, they accepted Ahmadinejad as the head of state.

The final opposition protest of the post-election period occurred on February 11, 2010, the 31st anniversary of the Islamic Revolution—a day traditionally reserved for pro-government rallies honoring the Islamic Revolution ("22 Bahman Protests: Iranian Opposition Planning Demonstrations on Anniversary of Revolution," 2010). Opposition activists led by the Green Movement and organized by the Coordinating Council of Reform Front, a coalition of 17 moderate political organizations, were called to gather publicly on that day.

15 These protests occurred on a day that always drew mass populations into the streets to commemorate the martyrdom of Hossein (see Betteridge, Kreyenbroek, and Hitchins, 1999). As such, it is difficult to determine how many of those marching were opposition protestors and how many marched for religious reasons.

As on prior occasions, Iran's chief of police warned opposition activists not to demonstrate, issuing a strongly worded statement that the government would be able to "identify anyone calling for rioting through text messaging" ("Iran: Opposition and Hard-Liners Get Ready for 22 Bahman Confrontations," 2010). The Green Movement protest failed to reach a critical mass. Rather, a government-sponsored rally attended by hundreds of thousands of government supporters drew all the attention that day (BBC News, 2010b).

CHAPTER FOUR

Overall Trends in Public Mood in Iran After the 2009 Presidential Election

In this chapter, we will first discuss the general indicators of public mood we examined across the nine months after the election. Specifically, these indicators show the extent to which people used emotion-laden words, such as swearing, anxiety words, and positive emotion words; first-person singular pronouns, which signify feelings of depression; and first-person plural, second-person (singular and plural), and third-person (singular and plural) pronouns, all of which signify a focus on interactions with others. To the fullest extent possible, we looked for patterns that occurred across multiple indicators at the same time, on the assumption that a trend in public mood is more robust if it affects more than one indicator of mood in written text. In addition to trends across time, we looked for spikes and dips in the indicators to determine whether these coincided with events on the ground. If they did, such a finding would shed light on how public mood shifted either during or in response to events on the ground.

Public Mood Throughout the Nine Months After the Election

Based on indicators of emotional states and interactive processes gleaned from the IranElection Twitter archive, one can gain an overall picture of how Twitter users' mood changed across the duration of the nine months following the election. At the outset, it is important to note an assumption we are making: that the usage of emotion words and pronouns by Twitter users (an unknown percentage of whom are Iranian, as discussed earlier) indicates the same psychological states and social processes that these words have been shown to indicate in Western contexts. Chapter Seven presents possible future directions for this research, which include testing the assumptions we have made in the current project.

In the remainder of this section, we show how patterns in word usage changed as protests took place inside Iran, to help readers understand how shifts in writing may have coincided with (or preceded) such protests. Given the events and protests that took place after the election, we examined the writing patterns people displayed through their tweets on the election, to determine what these patterns suggested about public mood. Although some indicators of public mood appeared to track better with events on the ground than others did, a picture emerged about this mood and the trends it might follow beyond the time period examined.

Twitter's Clearest Indicator of Mood and Forecaster of Action: Swear Words

Surprisingly, people's use of swear words on Twitter tracked more closely than any other indicator did with events and protests on the ground, and it did the best job of forecasting when protests would occur. Figure 4.1 plots the relative frequency of swearing in the IranElection

Twitter archive as a function of time; significant events in the election aftermath are noted at the top of the figure. For example, in the days after Khamenei's Friday prayer speech on June 19 and the shooting of Neda Soltan on June 20, people swore at significantly higher rates (i.e., during weeks 2–4, or June 21—July 11). As protests rocked the country throughout the month of July, people swore at their highest levels. However, as the government cracked down on protests and stopped them toward the end of July (possibly in preparation for Ahmadinejad's inauguration on August 3), people's rates of swearing dropped markedly—especially during the week after Ahmadinejad's inauguration (week 8, or August 2–8). Yet, people still swore at relatively elevated rates throughout the months of August and September, suggesting that they still felt angry during this time and might protest again—even though they stayed indoors during those weeks.

Indeed, by September 18, large-scale protests broke out again on Quds Day. After that day, the government cracked down more intensively than it had in the entire aftermath of election. At the same time that this crackdown took place (late September/early October), people reduced their swearing significantly, as Figure 4.1 shows. People swore at their lowest rates during the 20th week after the election (October 25–31), a time when no protests were reported on the ground. After that week, certain smaller-scale protests broke out, such as the November 4 anniversary of the takeover of the American embassy and the December 7 National Student Day protest. However, people did not swear at significantly higher rates again until two weeks before Ashura (i.e., during week 27 or December 13–19)—possibly foreshadowing the large-scale protests that would take place on Ashura. When the Ashura

Figure 4.1
Swearing on Twitter After the Election

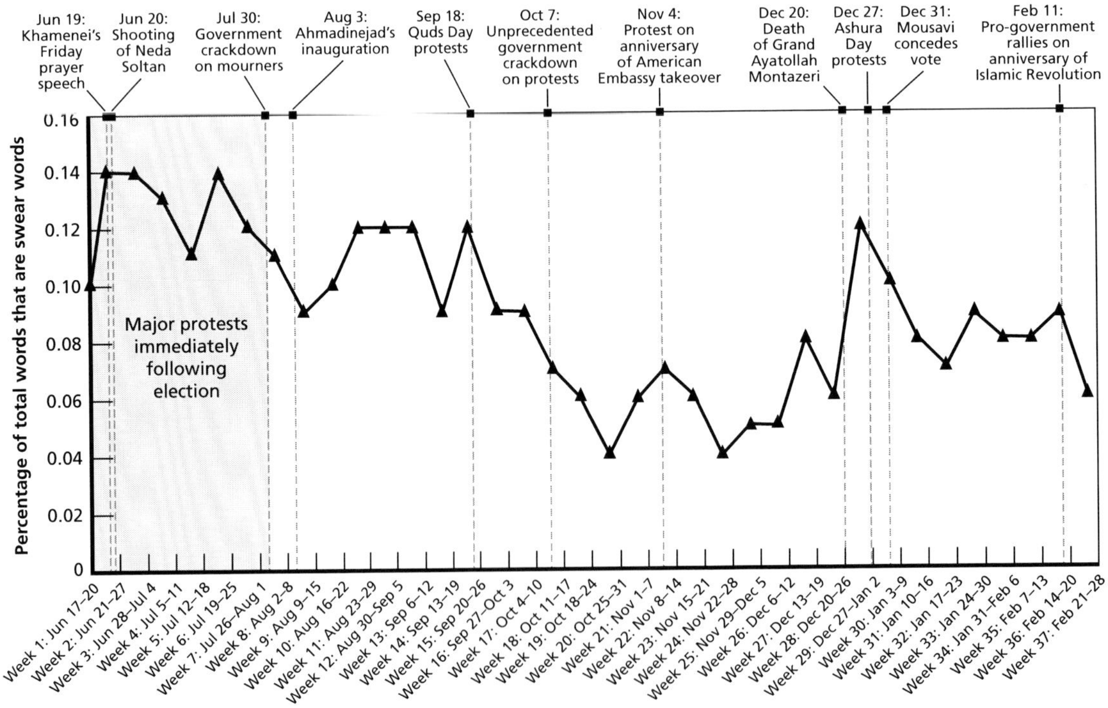

NOTES: The data points signify a ratio of the number of swear words to total words across an entire week's worth of tweets. Significant events in the aftermath of the election are noted at the top of the figure.

RAND *TR1161-4.1*

Day protests occured, people swore at high rates comparable to those in the initial aftermath of the election. However, after Ashura and the announcements by all three opposition leaders (Mousavi, Karroubi, and Khatami) that they accepted Ahmadinejad as the head of state, no other large-scale protests occurred. Indeed, throughout the rest of the time period examined, people reduced their swearing bit by bit, on average, and swearing dropped steeply after February 11, when pro-government rallies took place on the anniversary of the Islamic Revolution.

Based on this initial exploration of swearing rates and how they correspond with the outbreak of large-scale protests, it appears that swearing rates tended either to rise in the weeks before large-scale protests (such as before Ashura, December 27, 2009) or to stay elevated in the weeks before such protests (such as the Quds Day protest, September 18, 2009)—even when the streets were quiet. These results suggest that it may be possible to forecast large-scale events, such as protests, based on the extent to which people express anger through social media outlets. Additional studies, however, are needed to replicate the current results.

To understand more fully what people thought and felt as they swore on Twitter, we conducted an initial manual review of the tweets.[1] In particular, we sought to determine whether people actually used swear words in anger or whether they used these words in a positive way. Based on our initial review, we conclude that people often swore in anger at the Iranian government. Some examples of tweets include the following:

> Idea to punish khamenei: take the bullet fee and the bullet and shove it in his ass dollar by dollar 3000 times!

> ATTENTION: Very important message to all Basiji: FUCK YOU. yesterday we saw a 10 years old child die from teargas in his face - - could not film becos militia everywhere

Assuming that people's use of swear words does signify anger, the pattern of results suggests that as of the end of the period examined (i.e., by the end of February 2010), Twitter users may have felt resigned to their situation and would probably not further protest against the Iranian government in the short term following the post-election period. Another factor that could have contributed to this decreased swearing was fear of government retribution.

Use of Pronouns on Twitter After the Election

Pronouns constituted another set of indicators that tracked with events on the ground almost as well as swear words did. As discussed with regard to our methodology (see Chapter Two for an overview and the appendix for further detail), an extensive amount of research on how people react after traumatic events has focused on the way that they write and, specifically, their use of first-person, second-person, and third-person pronouns. Use of first-person singular pronouns (e.g., "I," "me," "mine") has been shown to signify a focus on one's self, which we interpreted in this context as generally negative or depressive states (Pennebaker and Chung, 2005, 2008), while use of first-person plural (e.g., "we," "us"), second-person singular or plural

---

[1] We reviewed every tweet posted in each of the time periods for which we observed significant changes in swearing. The only exception was in the several weeks immediately following the election, where the sheer volume of tweets made this impossible. For these time periods, we reviewed a selection of tweets at the beginning, middle, and end of the week. This approach, while not yielding a representative sample, should offer sufficient coverage of the tweets for the purposes of this initial study. We adopted this approach to examine all other indicators in this study. Future work should seek a more systematic approach to manually reviewing the tweets.

(e.g., "you," "your"), and third-person singular or plural (e.g., "he," "she," "they") signifies a focus on interactions with others.

Across each of the pronoun categories we examined over time, Twitter users followed similar patterns in their writing about the election. For the sake of clarity, we have depicted two pronoun trends in Figure 4.2 (out of a possible five that could have been depicted[2]): first-person singular pronouns and second-person (singular and plural) pronouns.

As Figure 4.2 shows, people increased their usage of first-person singular pronouns (signaling feelings of depression) from the second week after the election (June 21–27) to the fourth week after the election (July 5–11), even as they used elevated levels of second-person pronouns (signaling a desire to interact with others) throughout this period of mass protests. A combination of events on the ground may have caused people to increase their usage of first-person singular pronouns, such as the election, the protests that followed it, Khamenei's Friday prayer speech (on June 19—in which he asserted that the election had been free and fair and threatened the protestors), and/or the shooting of Neda Soltan (on June 20). At the same time, the relatively elevated usage of second-person pronouns suggests that people focused on their

Figure 4.2
Usage of First-Person Singular and Second-Person (Singular and Plural) Pronouns on Twitter After the Election

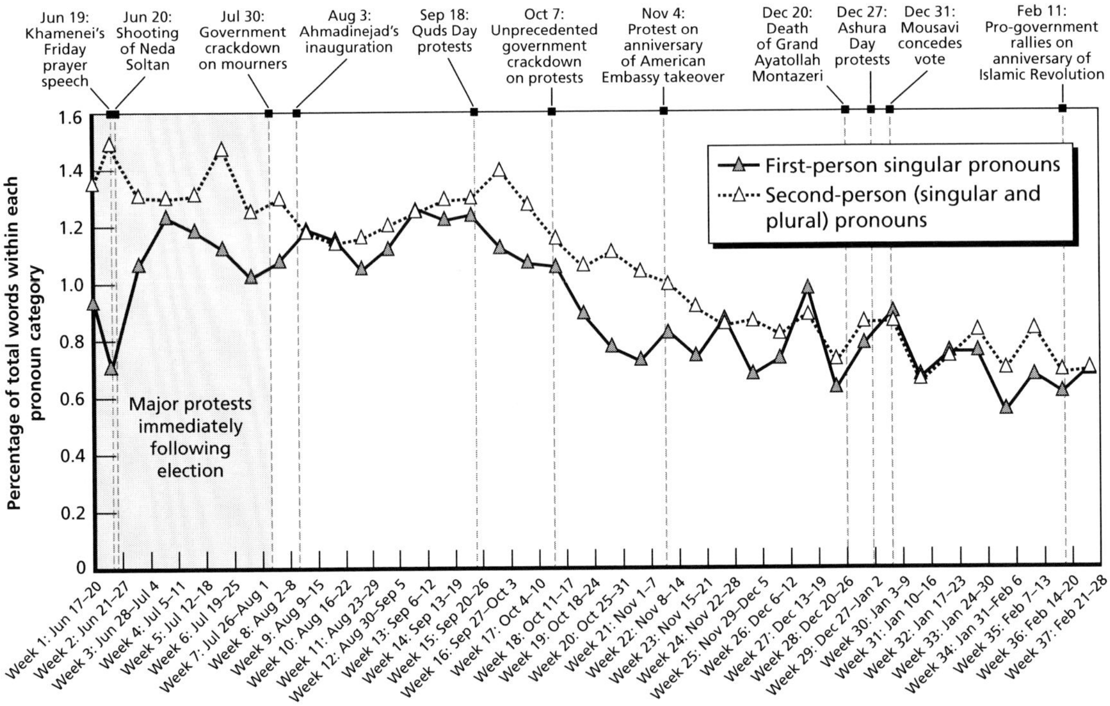

NOTES: The data points signify a ratio of the number of first-person singular and second-person (singular and plural) pronouns to total words across an entire week's worth of tweets. Significant events in the aftermath of the election are noted at the top of the figure.

RAND *TR1161-4.2*

---

[2] Although there are six pronoun categories (i.e., first-person, second-person, and third-person pronouns that include both singular and plural for each one), the total number of pronoun trends we could have depicted is five, because the second-person pronoun of "you" and all derivatives of it can be either singular or plural.

interactions with others in the social environment during these tense weeks after the election. Although usage of first-person singular pronouns dropped between the first week after the election (June 17–20) and the second week after the election (June 21–27), this drop did not appear large enough to be significant.

Between July 11 and October 3 (i.e., the end of the 16th week after the election), people continued to use relatively high levels of first-person singular and second-person (singular and plural) pronouns, suggesting a continued focus on themselves (and feelings of depression) as well as a tendency to reach out to others. Although large-scale protests ceased during the month of August and first two weeks of September, people's elevated use of both types of pronouns suggests that they continued to feel depressed and reach out to others. Among Twitter users inside Iran, the combination of these patterns suggests that they still felt dissatisfied with their circumstances and could potentially have been amenable to protesting at a later time. Therefore, based on this initial pattern of data, we would predict that those inside Iran using Twitter might resume their protests at some point, which is similar to the forecast obtained from swear words.

On September 18 (which was Quds Day—during the 14th week after the election), large-scale protests did resume. Furthermore, students kept protesting until the end of September. At the same time, Twitter users continued to write with relatively high rates of first-person singular and second-person singular and plural pronouns through September and slightly into October, but after that time, their usage of both types of pronouns dropped steadily until the end of February 2010.

The Quds protests were the last verifiably large-scale protests in Iran. By early October, the government began cracking down more intensely on the opposition by executing protestors for the first time, tightening its grip on the media and appointing two hard-line military veterans to security-related positions. It is possible that these harsher measures and others implemented over time might have caused many to accept that they could not change the situation through protests. If people resigned themselves to their situation as it was, they may have felt less depressed over time and less of a need to reach out to others, knowing that they would no longer challenge the government on a wide scale.

On the other hand, the gradual decline in pronoun usage from the end of the Quds Day protests until the end of February contradicts our findings regarding swear words, which spiked before, during, and after Ashura Day (December 27). It is impossible to know how large the Ashura Day protest really was, and it may not have been large enough for the pronoun indicators to "register" it. The swear-word indicator appears to have been the more sensitive one, as it registered mounting public anger before Ashura Day.

It should be noted that, just as with swear words, people decreased their use of first-person singular and second-person (singular and plural) pronouns after the Ashura protests (December 27) and opposition leader statements accepting Ahmadinejad as head of state (late December through January) to the end of the period examined (i.e., February 28). As with the swear-word indicator, this finding suggests that Twitter users inside Iran may have felt resigned about the election, unlikely to protest again in the near future.

This conclusion illustrates one of the uses of the current methodology for intelligence analysts. That is, this methodology can help analysts make informed assessments of public opinion in certain countries by examining the nature of what people write on social media. Because writing styles are linked with mood states and tendencies to either reach out to others or withdraw, analysts can gain some understanding of psychological dynamics on the ground in countries of interest.

Although only first-person singular and second-person (singular and plural) pronouns are depicted in Figure 4.2, other pronouns followed similar patterns as those described above. For example, people's usage of first-person plural pronouns (i.e., "we, us, our") peaked in late September (and specifically, in the days after Quds Day). The point at which usage of first-person plural pronouns started declining coincided with the government's more intensive crackdown on protesters. In fact, people's usage of these pronouns declined, on average, throughout the rest of the time period examined. To the extent that usage of first-person plural pronouns signifies a focus on interacting with others in one's own group, people may have felt less of a need for such interaction as they accepted the reality of what had occurred.

With regard to third-person plural pronouns (e.g., "they," "them," "their," etc.), people used the highest rates of these in the earliest weeks after the election but gradually used fewer of them across the nine months examined. It is possible that, during the earliest phases of the protests, people made the most references to government figures and what "they" might have been doing at the time. As previous research shows, people use third-person plural pronouns to refer to an oppositional group or government in certain contexts (Pennebaker and Chung, 2008). With the passage of time and possible acclimation to their circumstances, however, Iranians using Twitter may not have felt as much of a need to make such references. Interestingly, with regard to third-person singular pronouns (e.g., "she," "he," etc.), people gradually increased their usage of these until mid-August; after this point, they reduced their usage, on average, throughout the rest of the time period (similar to the third-person plural pronouns).

Summary

- Linguistic trends that indicated anger, depression, and a need to reach out to others suggested that, as of the end of February 2010, the opposition movement would probably not protest against the government in the near future and had probably resigned itself to the political situation in the short term.
- Across the nine months after the election, Twitterers' usage of swear words forecasted when large-scale protests would occur.
- Twitterers' usage of pronouns served as nearly an effective predictor of protests as swear words did.

CHAPTER FIVE

Iranian Public Opinion About Specific Topics in the Aftermath of the 2009 Election

Having explored overall public mood across the nine months after the election, we turn to more specific indicators of public opinion regarding political figures in Iran, including the candidates who ran for president during the 2009 election. These individuals include Supreme Leader Ayatollah Ali Khamenei, President Mahmoud Ahmadinejad, leading electoral contender Mir Hussein Mousavi, and electoral contender Mehdi Karroubi. Because we could not find relevant prior work on social media in the Iranian context, and because of ambiguities surrounding our sample, we did not pose specific hypotheses regarding public opinion on these figures. Rather, we took a "bottom-up" approach to examine the patterns in people's writing about these figures and to determine what these patterns might suggest about public opinion about them, more broadly.

Public Opinion Leading Domestic Political Figures: Ahmadinejad, Khamenei, Mousavi, and Karroubi

Summary

- Twitter users felt angrier at President Ahmadinejad than at leading opposition candidate Mousavi in the initial weeks after the election. But this pattern had reversed itself by the end of the period examined, with Twitter users feeling angrier at Mousavi than at Ahmadinejad when the opposition movement had flagged (by February 2010).
- During the same time period (February 2010), the results suggest that Twitter users felt angrier at Mousavi than at Karroubi, possibly because Mousavi had been the frontrunner in the election.
- Multiple results suggest that linguistic indicators can pinpoint gaps in existing knowledge of how events inside Iran affect people's perceptions of political figures and topics. Intelligence analysts can use such gaps to target collection assets.
  - For example, three linguistic indicators showed that people felt more negatively about Khamenei than Ahmadinejad at the time of the Quds Day protests, but it is not clear why.
  - An indicator of positive emotions showed that people felt more positively about Karroubi than about Mousavi after Quds Day, but, once again, it is not clear why.

Background

Supreme Leader Ayatollah Ali Khamenei. As Supreme Leader, Ayatollah Ali Khamenei is Iran's highest political, military, and religious authority. He is conservative in outlook and ideologically and politically opposed to the United States. He has been Iran's Supreme Leader since 1989; prior to that, he occupied a number of other positions, including president of the Islamic Republic.

Although he is Iran's ultimate authority, Khamenei is nevertheless constitutionally required to share power with Iran's elected institutions, including the presidency and the Majles (Parliament). However, Khamenei has accumulated even greater power through the support of the Revolutionary Guards and President Mahmoud Ahmadinejad. The two men share a common ideological and political outlook, including "resistance" to the United States. Khamenei's decisive support for Ahmadinejad in the 2009 election sparked massive demonstrations throughout Iran and may have led to a loss of Khamenei's credibility as a fair arbitrator of Iran's political system (Sadjadpour, 2008).

President Mahmoud Ahmadinejad. President Ahmadinejad was elected Iran's president in 2005 and again in 2009. He has used his humble beginnings and social class to gain a degree of popularity. Ahmadinejad has been heavily supported by the Revolutionary Guards and the Basij, in addition to Khamenei. Many of his supporters are believed to hail from the rural and urban lower classes. He believes in a return to the "principles" of the Islamic Revolution and has harshly criticized the "corruption" of Iran's traditional elite, including former president Ayatollah Akbar Hashemi Rafsanjani. Ahmadinejad is fiercely opposed to the reformist socio-political agenda and, by extension, the Green Movement. He has also pursued a strident nuclear policy in the face of U.S. and international pressure.

Mir Hussein Mousavi. Mir Hussein Mousavi is the most visible and arguably most influential leader of the Green Movement. He served as Iran's Prime Minister from 1981 to 1989 (before the position was eliminated). A committed and leftist revolutionary, Mousavi led the Islamic Republic though the tumultuous Iran-Iraq War. After his premiership, Mousavi largely disappeared from public view, only to reappear on the political stage before the 2009 election. By then Mousavi had lost much of his ideological zeal and had taken up the reformist mantle. He led a well-organized campaign targeting women and Iranian youth; his outspoken wife, Zahra Rahnavard, campaigned beside him. Mousavi has repeatedly claimed fraud in the 2009 elections and believes that he should have been the rightful winner. He instigated the massive protests that took place in Tehran and beyond and has led the Green Movement since the election. His physical movements and ability to lead the Green Movement were circumscribed by the state's security forces (Sadjadpour, 2008).

Mehdi Karroubi. A mid-ranking cleric, Mehdi Karroubi was one of the original revolutionary leaders and founding members of the Islamic Republic. A confidante of Ayatollah Khomeini, Karroubi was the speaker of parliament from 1989 to 1992 and 2000 to 2004. He has been closely associated with the reformist movement that elected Mohammad Khatami as president in 1997. Karroubi has led his own party and faction of the movement, however, and has been more outspoken than either Mousavi or Khatami. He became a leader of the Green Movement after the 2009 election and has been repeatedly threatened and assaulted by state security forces. He not only has claimed the election to have been null and void, but has directly attacked the judgment and even authority of the Supreme Leader (Sadjadpour, 2008).

Comparing Trends in Public Opinion About Political Figures

To analyze public opinion about each of these leaders as expressed through Twitter, we compared trends in emotion word usage for two leaders at a time. One reason for comparing trends is that it is easier to interpret a trend for any given leader when comparing it with a trend for another leader than when viewing it in isolation. There are also substantive reasons for doing so: for example, this would allow one to determine which of two figures was more popular. We examined three pairs of trends: those for (1) President Ahmadinejad and Supreme Leader Khamenei, (2) leading opposition candidate Mir Hussein Mousavi and candidate Mehdi Karroubi, and (3) President Ahmadinejad and leading opposition candidate Mousavi.

To select pairs of leaders for comparison, we first turned to leaders of the current government: Supreme Leader Khamenei and President Ahmadinejad. Although analysts and commentators know what each leader said and did over the nine months following the election, it is less clear how individuals using social media—especially Twitter—viewed each leader in comparison with each other over the nine months following the election. It is also unknown whether emotions became more extreme—in either a positive direction or a negative one—for either leader at various points in time. Examining the spikes and dips that may have occurred in emotionally expressive writing for each leader at different points in time can also serve to pinpoint when some event may have occurred to cause such spikes or dips for each leader.

After focusing on leaders of the current government, we next turned to opinion on the two primary opposition candidates: Mir Hussein Mousavi and Mehdi Karroubi. As with the government leaders, we examined whether spikes and/or dips in emotional content over time served to pinpoint some occurrence worthy of further examination.

Finally, as a methodological demonstration, we compared emotional expressions regarding President Ahmadinejad with expressions regarding the leading electoral contender, Mousavi. In this case, we predicted that people using social media would express more negative emotions regarding President Ahmadinejad than Mousavi because of the widespread protests that took place during this period. Results supporting this prediction would serve to validate the indicators of emotion being tested.

Around the Quds Day Protest, Twitter Users Wrote More Negatively About Khamenei Than About Ahmadinejad

Our first set of comparative analyses focused on President Ahmadinejad and Supreme Leader Khamenei. Three of LIWC's linguistic indicators revealed a similar pattern of writing about these leaders at a specific, significant point in time given events on the ground. Namely, during the 16th week after the election (September 27–October 3), the widespread Quds Day protests took place. Three indicators showed that people wrote more negatively about Supreme Leader Khamenei than about President Ahmadinejad at this time. That is, LIWC's indicator of "anxiety" words revealed a spike in certain words surrounding Khamenei that rose significantly higher than a simultaneous increase of these words surrounding Ahmadinejad (see Figure 5.1). A manual inspection of tweets from this period containing the word "Khamenei" as well word(s) from LIWC's "anxiety" category shows that people used the word "ashamed" with regard to Khamenei more than any of the other "anxiety" words. Some examples of these tweets are:

Figure 5.1
Comparing Usage of "Anxiety" Words When Writing About Khamenei and Ahmadinejad

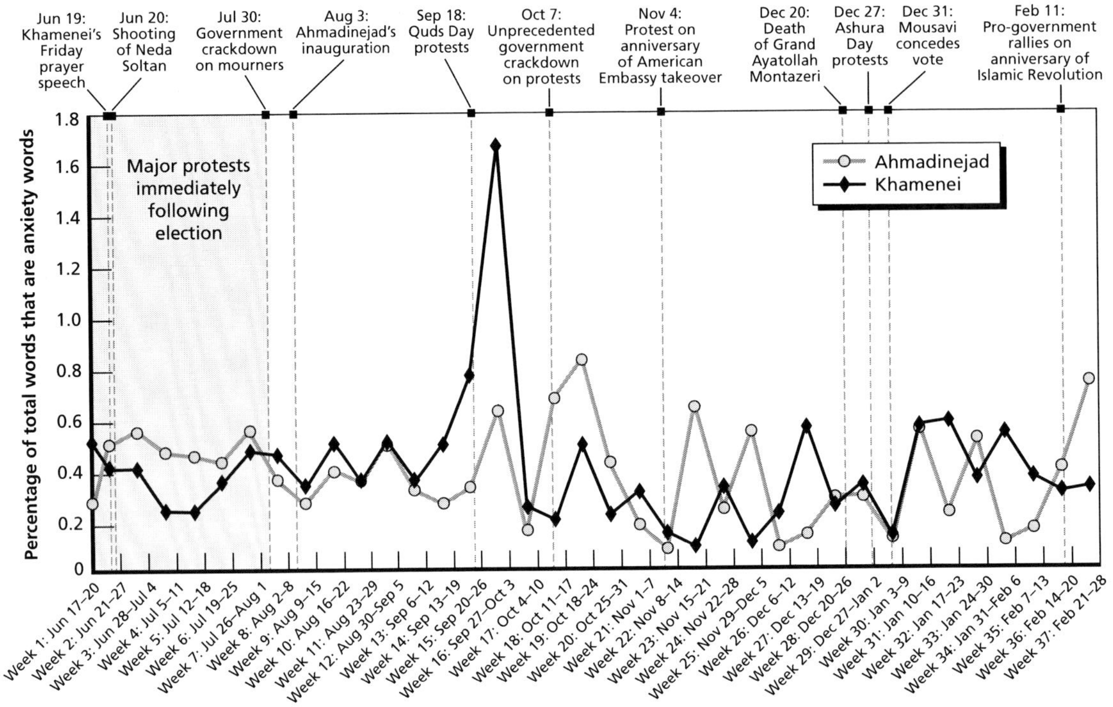

NOTES: The data points signify a ratio of the number of anxiety words to total words across an entire week's worth of tweets. Significant events in the aftermath of the election are noted at the top of the figure.
RAND *TR1161-5.1*

> Mr. Khamenei I Wish You'd Feel Ashamed Of Yourself[1]
>
> Shah was the shame of Iran as the Khomeini and Khamenei

In this case, use of the words "ashamed" and "shame" do not appear to signify anxiety per se, but they indicate some other negative emotion, such as disdain or anger. The issue of classifying and labeling certain words in particular contexts will be discussed at the end of this chapter.

In addition to using more disdainful (or angry) language regarding Khamenei than Ahmadinejad at the time of the Quds Day protests, Twitterers also used more first-person singular pronouns (signifying feelings of depression) when writing about Khamenei at this time than when writing about Ahmadinejad (see Figure 5.2).

Finally, Twitterers swore at higher rates about Khamanei than about Ahmadinejad during the week of the Quds Day protests (as well as at other times—see Figure 5.3). This pattern suggests that Twitterers felt angrier at Khamenei than at Ahmadinejad during the week of Quds Day.

Although three different linguistic indicators suggest that Twitterers felt worse about Khamenei than about Ahmadinejad at the time of the Quds Day protests, it is not immedi-

1 This tweet was retweeted most frequently. Retweets should have minimal negative impact on analyses; the fact that they were sent out in place of an individual's own words suggests some degree of approval and overlap with the individual's own opinions and attitudes.

Figure 5.2
Comparing Usage of First-Person Singular Pronouns When Writing About Khamenei and Ahmadinejad

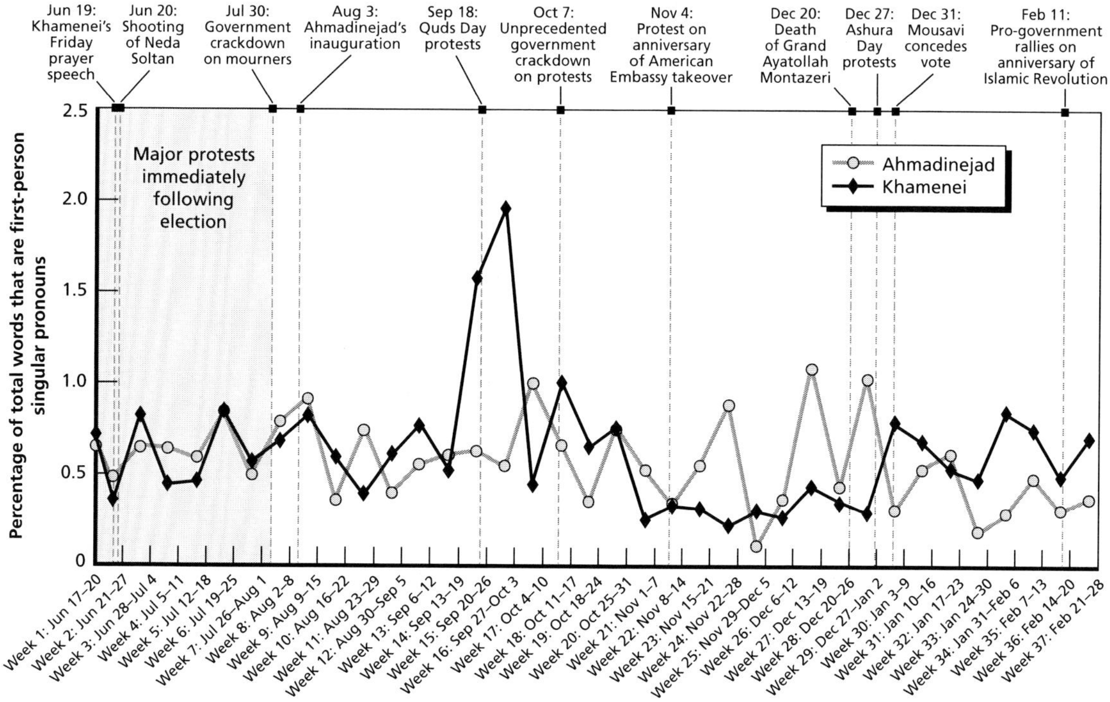

NOTES: The data points signify a ratio of the number of first-person singular pronouns to total words across an entire week's worth of tweets. Significant events in the aftermath of the election are noted at the top of the figure.
RAND *TR1161-5.2*

ately obvious from existing information sources examined why this would be the case. As such, one possible usage of the linguistic indicators presented may be to pinpoint gaps in analysts' and policymakers' understanding of factors that may have shaped public opinion regarding political leaders or other topics. Such information gaps could even point toward areas where the intelligence community can target collection assets.

At Certain Points, Twitter Users Wrote More Positively and Less Negatively About Karroubi Than About Mousavi

After comparing trends in the way that Twitter users wrote about Khamenei and Ahmadinejad, we examined whether they distinguished between the two opposition candidates, Mousavi and Karroubi, in any way or at any point in time. An inspection of all indicators and a manual sampling of tweets that they represent showed that two indicators revealed meaningful differences in the way Twitterers wrote about Mousavi and Karroubi. These were the positive-emotion indicator and, once again, the swear-word indicator.

Interestingly, as with our analysis of writing on Khamenei and Ahmadinejad, the positive emotion indicator revealed significant differences in the way people wrote about Mousavi and Karroubi just after the Quds Day protest (i.e., during the 15th week after the election, or September 20–26). As Figure 5.4 shows, expressions of positive emotion spiked for Karroubi during this time in a way that they did not for Mousavi. Furthermore, a manual inspection of

Figure 5.3
Comparison of Swearing About Khamenei and Ahmadinejad Over Time

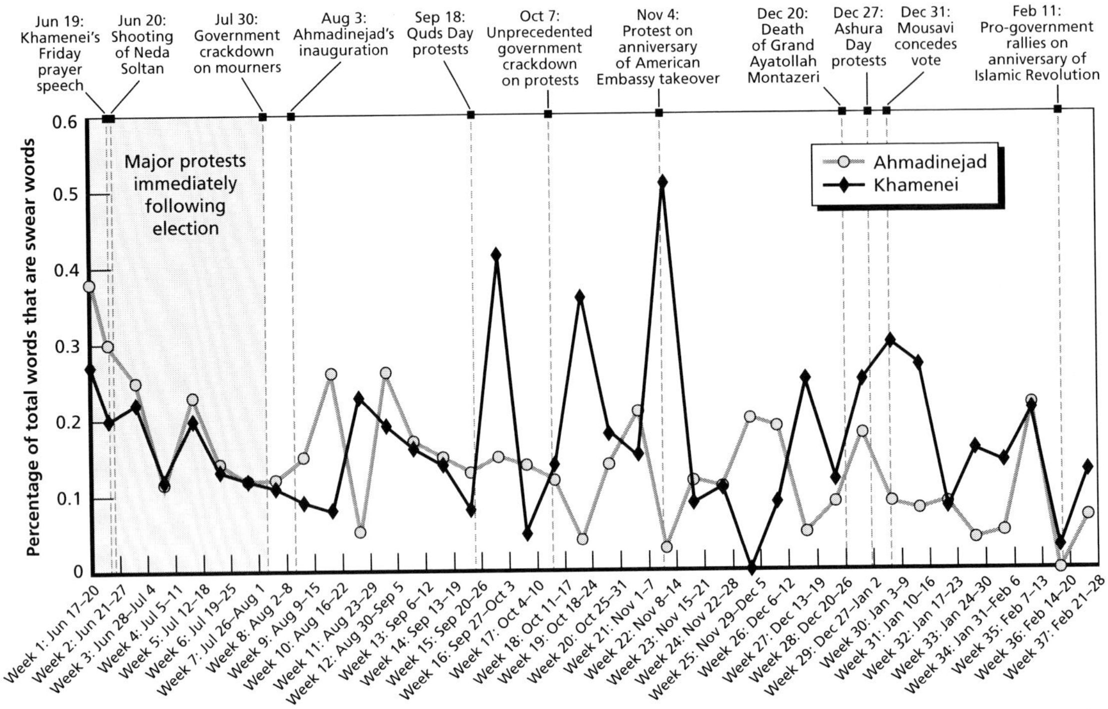

NOTES: The data points signify a ratio of the number of swear words to total words across an entire week's worth of tweets. Significant events in the aftermath of the election are noted at the top of the figure.
RAND *TR1161-5.3*

tweets collected during week 15 suggests that the indicator tapped positive emotion. We present excerpts of these tweets here:

> clap clap clap KARROUBI! clap clap clap KARROUBI! clap clap clap KARROUBI! clap clap clap retweet
>
> I LOVE KARROUBI! I LOVE KARROUBI! I LOVE KARROUBI! BRAVE FIGHTER RISKING ALL for THE PPL! (Yes I'm YELLING!)
>
> Twitition to nominate Obi Wan Karroubi for Nobel Peace Prize
>
> Karroubi is doing his best 2help Ppl He is standing for justice Stand with him Please support Karroubi UR support may give him some Protection
>
> Yah and please hold Karroubi signs in GreenNY too! He's the true supporter of Iranians! Mousavi is 2nd.

Although the results suggest that expressions of positive emotion spiked more for Karroubi than for Mousavi in the days after the Quds Day protest, it is, once again, not clear why this would happen after Quds Day. Butters (2009), in *Time Magazine*, makes a case that despite the fact that Karroubi finished last in Iran's disputed presidential election, he often took the lead in challenging the Iranian government in the weeks that followed. For example,

Figure 5.4
Comparison of Positive-Emotion Expressions for Karroubi and Mousavi Over Time

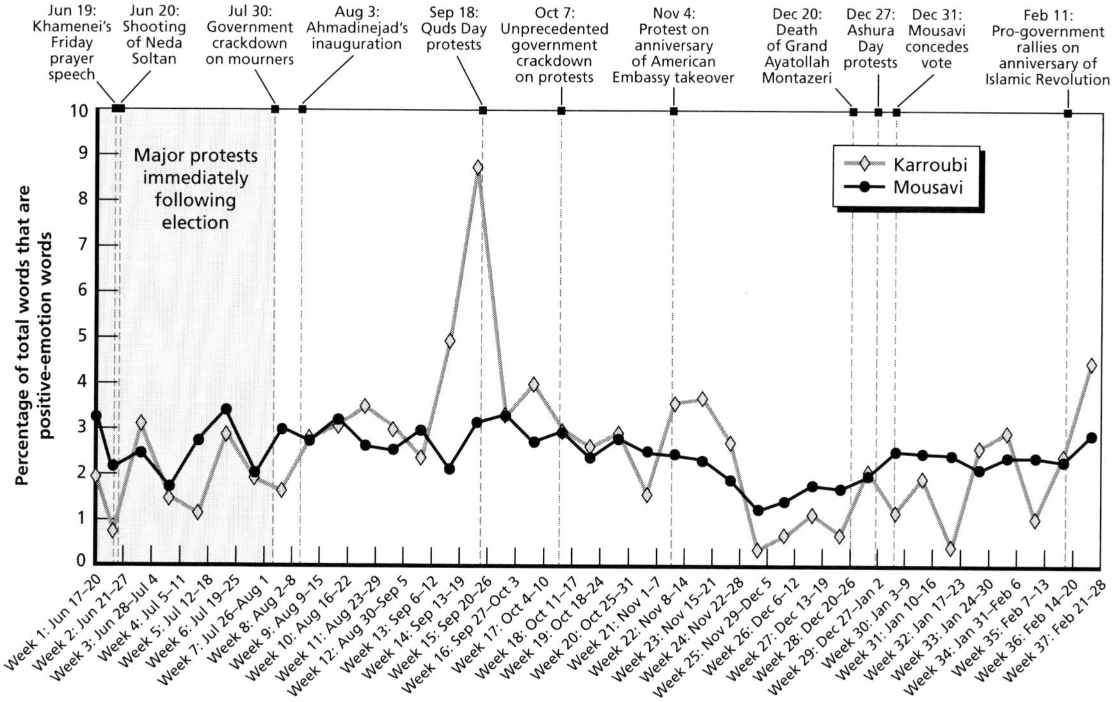

NOTES: The data points signify a ratio of the positive-emotion expressions to total words across an entire week's worth of tweets. Significant events in the aftermath of the election are noted at the top of the figure.
RAND *TR1161-5.4*

after the announcement of the result caused massive demonstrations in June, Karroubi became one of the first to blame the government for the violence. Later on, he publicized the charge that prison guards raped and abused opposition protesters. This view contended that although Mousavi became the opposition frontrunner in large part because he was the best-known reformist in the race, his popularity stemmed largely from the fact that he is not Ahmadinejad. On the other hand, reports noted that Karroubi, though less well known, ran on a program of reforms targeted at specific electoral groups, such as women, students, and the non-Persian minorities who make up almost half of Iran's population. Although these contentions suggest why Karroubi may have garnered significant popularity, there is still no obvious answer to the question of why positive emotion for Karroubi spiked in the days after Quds Day (as opposed to other times). Iran analysts and policymakers might therefore use such an indicator to identify gaps in existing knowledge.

In addition to the positive-emotion indicator, the swear-word indicator revealed significant differences in writing styles with regard to Mousavi and Karroubi. Specifically, Figure 5.5 shows that people gradually swore more about Mousavi in general as time went on, and, for the most part, they swore more about him than about Karroubi. Toward the end of the time period examined (i.e., the 33rd week after the election, corresponding to January 24–30, 2010, and the 35th week after the election, corresponding to February 7–13, 2010), swearing spiked for Mousavi in a way that it did not for Karroubi. At that time, the opposition movement appeared to have flagged in the sense that it could no longer rally a significant number of people to demonstrate on February 11, the anniversary of the Islamic Revolution. As discussed above, the

Figure 5.5
Comparison of Swearing About Mousavi and Karroubi Over Time

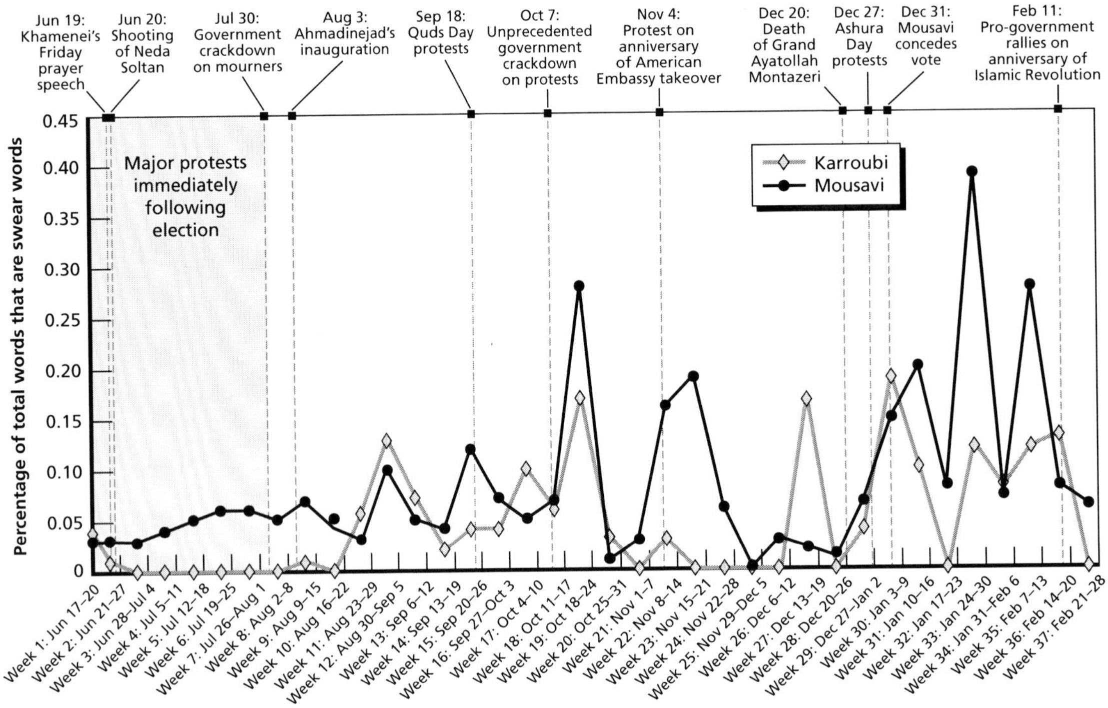

NOTES: The data points signify a ratio of the swear words to total words across an entire week's worth of tweets. Significant events in the aftermath of the election are noted at the top of the figure.
RAND *TR1161-5.5*

rallies that took place that day consisted mostly of government supporters. Given what happened on the ground, it is perhaps not surprising that Twitter users might curse Mousavi (the opposition frontrunner in the election). A manual inspection of tweets from these time periods shows that people did curse directly about Mousavi, in the context of expressing frustration with his absence or silence.

The fact that Twitter users cursed Mousavi substantially more than Karroubi by the end of the period examined highlights another use of the current methodology for intelligence analysts. Namely, this methodology can help intelligence analysts assess the impact of political events or actions on public opinion. In this case, the point at which the opposition movement appeared to wane corresponded with a rise in swearing about Mousavi, suggesting that people might have vented anger toward Mousavi in connection with the weakening opposition movement. Although it is impossible to draw a causal link between the waning opposition movement and anger at Mousavi, such results can be suggestive of a connection.

Initially, Twitter Users Swore More About Ahmadinejad Than About Mousavi, but the Opposite Became True

Finally, as a methodological demonstration, we tested the hypothesis that Twitter users would write more negatively about Ahmadinejad than about the leading opposition candidate, Mousavi, in the aftermath of the election. As with several other topics examined in this report, the swear-word indicator showed that, indeed, Twitterers swore significantly more about Ahmadinejad than about Mousavi in the initial weeks after the election (see Figure 5.6).

Figure 5.6
Comparison of Swearing About Ahmadinejad and Mousavi Over Time

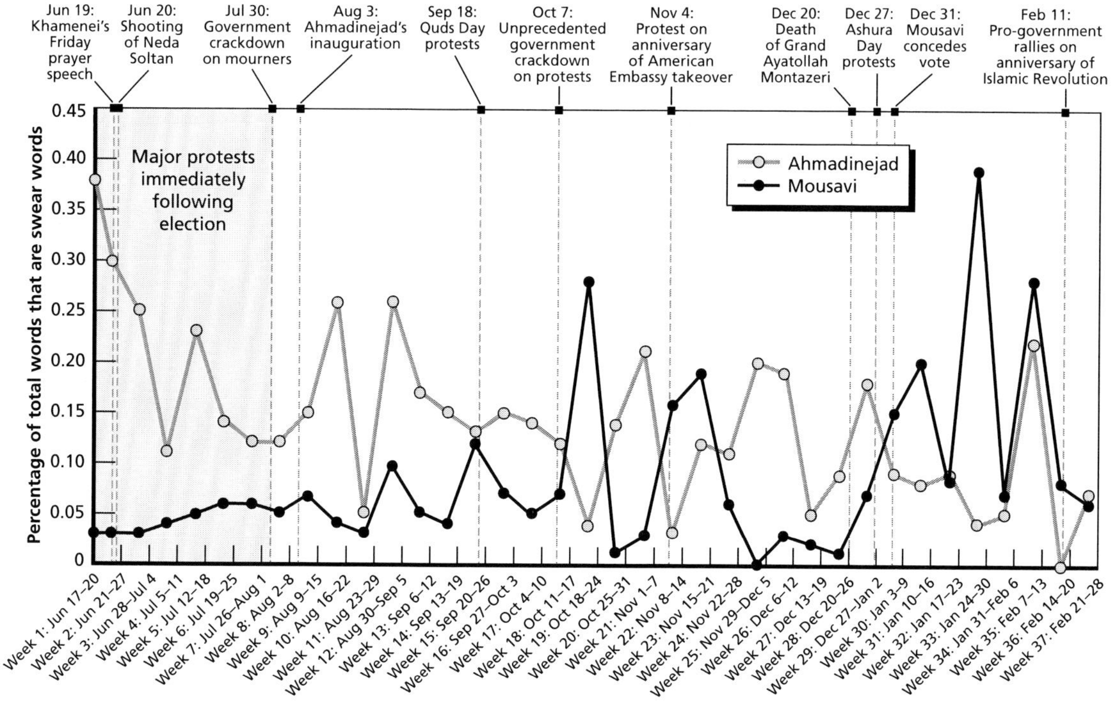

NOTES: The data points signify a ratio of the swear words to total words across an entire week's worth of tweets. Significant events in the aftermath of the election are noted at the top of the figure.
RAND *TR1161-5.6*

A manual inspection of the swear words people used in the first week after the election shows that they were directly cursing Ahmadinejad more than Mousavi.

Interestingly, though, people's swearing rates followed an approximate "crossover" pattern that we did not predict, such that in the weeks after the Ashura protests (when the opposition movement appeared to have flagged), people swore about Mousavi more than about Ahmadinejad. These results may reveal how particular events drive public opinion. On the one hand, the fact that Twitter users swore about Ahmadinejad in the early weeks after the election suggests that the election impacted public opinion negatively toward him. On the other hand, the fact that Twitter users swore more frequently about Mousavi than about Ahmadinejad in the second half of the period examined suggests that the weakening opposition movement caused people eventually to feel angrier at Mousavi.

Policy Implications

Our examination of how Twitter users wrote about the Iranian election yielded certain implications for policymakers. Chief among these is that multiple linguistic trends (such as those indicating anger, a sense of depression, and a need to reach out to others) suggest that, as of the end of February 2010, the opposition movement would probably not protest against the government in the short term following the post-election period. In addition, the results suggest that Twitterers felt angrier at Ahmadinejad than at Mousavi in the initial weeks after the election. This pattern, however, reversed itself by the end of the period examined, suggesting that Twitterers felt angrier at Mousavi than at Ahmadinejad when the opposition movement had waned. During the same time period when the opposition lost momentum, the results suggest that Twitterers felt angrier at Mousavi than at Karroubi, possibly because Mousavi had been the frontrunner in the election.

Of potential use to intelligence analysts, Twitterers' usage of profanity appeared to forecast when large-scale protests would occur. In addition, their use of pronouns served as nearly an effective forecaster of protests as swear words did. Multiple results suggest that linguistic indicators can pinpoint where information is lacking about events in Iran and how such events affect people's perceptions of political figures and topics. For example, three linguistic indicators showed that people felt worse about Khamenei than Ahmadinejad at the time of the Quds Day protests, but it is not clear why. In addition, an indicator of positive emotions showed that people felt better about Karroubi than about Mousavi after Quds Day, but the causes are again unclear. As such, the intelligence community could use indicators such as these to decide how to target collection assets.

Pro-Government and Opposition Groups: The Green Movement, the Revolutionary Guards, and the Basij

Summary

- Twitter users expressed considerable positive emotion toward the Green Movement in the initial weeks after the election, but this positive regard dropped steeply after then and remained low across the rest of the time period examined.
- Nonetheless, Twitterers consistently expressed more positive emotion toward the Green Movement than toward the IRGC and Basij across the entire time period examined.
- For both the IRGC and Basij, Twitterers expressed consistently low amounts of positive emotion throughout the entire period.
- Twitterers expressed more anger at the Basij militia, on the whole, than at the IRGC.

Background

The Green Movement. The Green Movement developed after the disputed 2009 presidential election (Milani, 2010). This movement has been viewed as a nonviolent, non-utopian, and populist paradigm of revolution that combined 21st century Internet technology with the power of people in the street. In the months after the election, the Green Movement evolved from a mass group of angry voters to a nationwide force demanding democratic rights originally sought in the 1979 revolution. Every few weeks, protesters took to the streets to challenge the regime and its leadership. However, by early 2010, the regime had crushed such displays of opposition. The Green Movement, therefore, retreated into a period of soul-searching and regrouping.

The Islamic Revolutionary Guards Corps (IRGC). The IRGC is Iran's most powerful economic, social, and political institution ("Islamic Revolutionary Guards Corps," 2009). It was created at the founding of the Islamic Republic as an elite military force, but its broad mandate—to protect the revolution—has allowed it to act far beyond its military role. In the aftermath of the 2009 presidential election, the IRGC emerged as a driving force to put down the opposition movement, according to media reports (Slackman, 2009a). For example, senior Guards officials acquired important government positions after the post-election protests. In addition, the IRGC used privatization as a way of extending their reach at home. According to Iranian analysts, the IRGC's ability to enhance its status since the election has important implications for the future of Iran's domestic politics, nuclear decisionmaking, and prospects for long-term relations with the West (Slackman, 2009a). Increasingly, the IRGC's interests and those of its allies are driving Iran's policies, and those interests have often been defined by isolation from the West.

The Basij. Serving under the IRGC's leadership, the Basij is a set of pro-government militarized organizations ("Basij Militia," 2009). These organizations range from more official units, such as the Ansar Hezbollah, which undergo formal training, to many groups controlled by local clerics. The word *basij* translates roughly as "mass mobilization" in Persian, and the original organization contained all the civilian volunteers whom Ayatollah Khomeini urged to fight on the front in the Iran-Iraq war. It is not known how many people belong to the Basij, but estimates run from a few hundred thousand to more than 1 million.

Mir Hussein Mousavi, an opposition presidential candidate, decried the Basij's violent actions in the wake of the disputed election, but he did not name the group directly. Noting that the Basijis lack uniforms, proper identification, or anything that marks them as public employees, he said they appeared with hoses, clubs, iron bars, truncheons, and sometimes firearms.

Comparing Trends in Public Opinion About Political Groups

To gain a deeper understanding of how people felt about the Green Movement, the IRGC, and its subsidiary Basij forces, we juxtaposed trends for each of these groups against each other.[2]

The Green Movement Was Viewed More Positively Than the Revolutionary Guards or Basij

Twitterers wrote the most positive expressions about the Green Movement in the initial weeks after the election (see Figure 5.7). During week 4 (July 5–11), specifically, the most common positive-emotion words that Twitterers used regarding the Green Movement were "peace" and "support." Examples of tweets with these words appear below:

> Noble Peace Prize for Green Movement/Mousavi Please retweet

> Peace justice humanity dignity trust isn't that what the green movement is really about?

> The GREEN movement needs the support of all Iranians irrespective of ideology. please SUPPORT those who support GREEN Movement!

After this initial outpouring of support for the Green Movement, the trend in positive emotion words leveled off, remaining relatively consistent and low throughout the rest of the period examined. This trend suggests that Twitterers grew disillusioned with the Green Movement relatively early on, or at least that they did not feel as enthusiastic about it as before. Nonetheless, Twitterers wrote with more consistently positive emotional expressions about the Green Movement than they did about either the IRGC or its subsidiary Basij forces. When

---

[2] We also examined the phrase "Revolutionary Guards" but could not use it in the analyses discussed here. For our analysis of positive emotions expressed, the positive emotion indicator did not validly track such emotions in connection with the phrase "Revolutionary Guards" (based on an initial inspection of the tweets). Regarding our analysis of swear words expressed, almost no swear words appeared in connection with the phrase "Revolutionary Guards."

Figure 5.7
Expression of Positive Emotions in Connection with the Green Movement, IRGC, and Basij

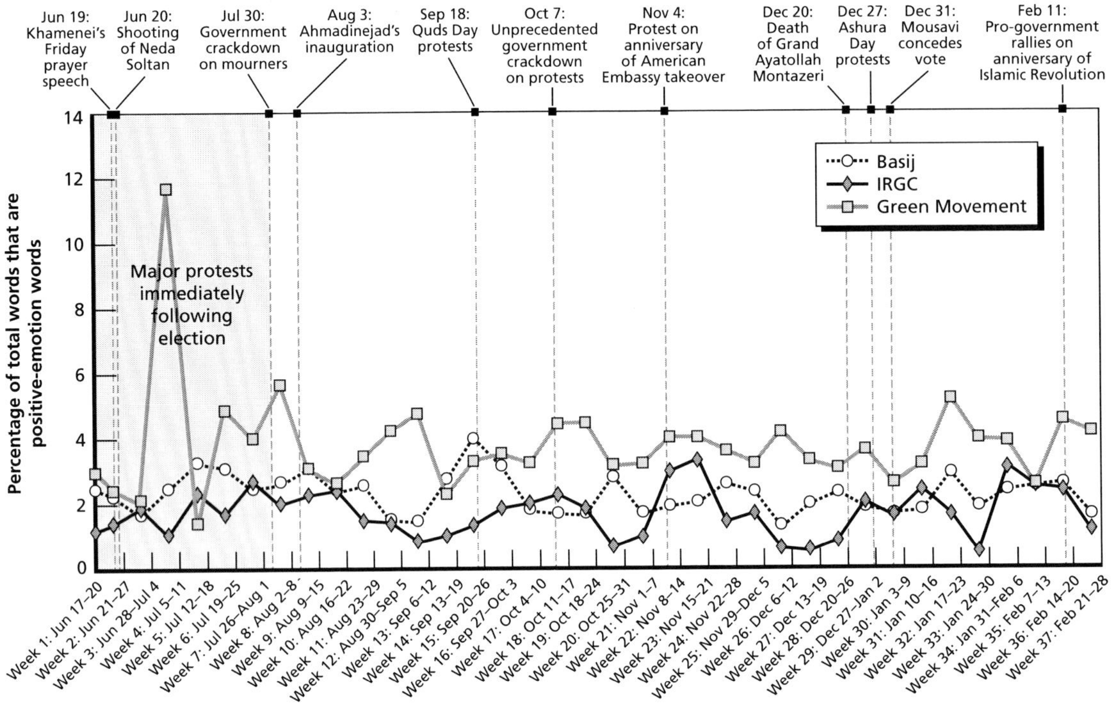

NOTES: The data points signify a ratio of the positive-emotion expressions to total words across an entire week's worth of tweets. Significant events in the aftermath of the election are noted at the top of the figure.
RAND *TR1161-5.7*

it came to both pro-government forces, people wrote with relatively few positive emotional expressions throughout the entire period examined. However, when it came to the negative expressions that people used in their tweets, people appeared to write particularly negatively about the Basij. For example,

> Why did the Basij cross the road? Cause he was a chicken? No Just following orders - what did he do there - killed unarmed people

Twitter Users Swore More About the Basij Than About the Revolutionary Guards

Both the IRGC and Basij made headlines with their use of violent tactics against the opposition movement. On top of committing such violence, the IRGC tightened its financial and political grip on society by placing IRGC leaders in senior government positions and by taking control of Iran's telecommunications industry. Yet when it came to writing about both groups on Twitter, people expressed more anger toward the Basij than the IRGC. For example, Figure 5.8 depicts how people swore about the Basij as opposed to the IRGC.

Twitterers swore at higher rates about the Basij than the IRGC in the earliest weeks after the election as well as at several points throughout the time period examined. An initial manual inspection of the tweets suggests that Twitterers swore about the Basij directly and that the swear-word indicator reflected public anger toward this set of militias. Some examples of these tweets are the following (from week 6, or July 19–25):

Figure 5.8
Swearing About the IRGC and Basij After the 2009 Election

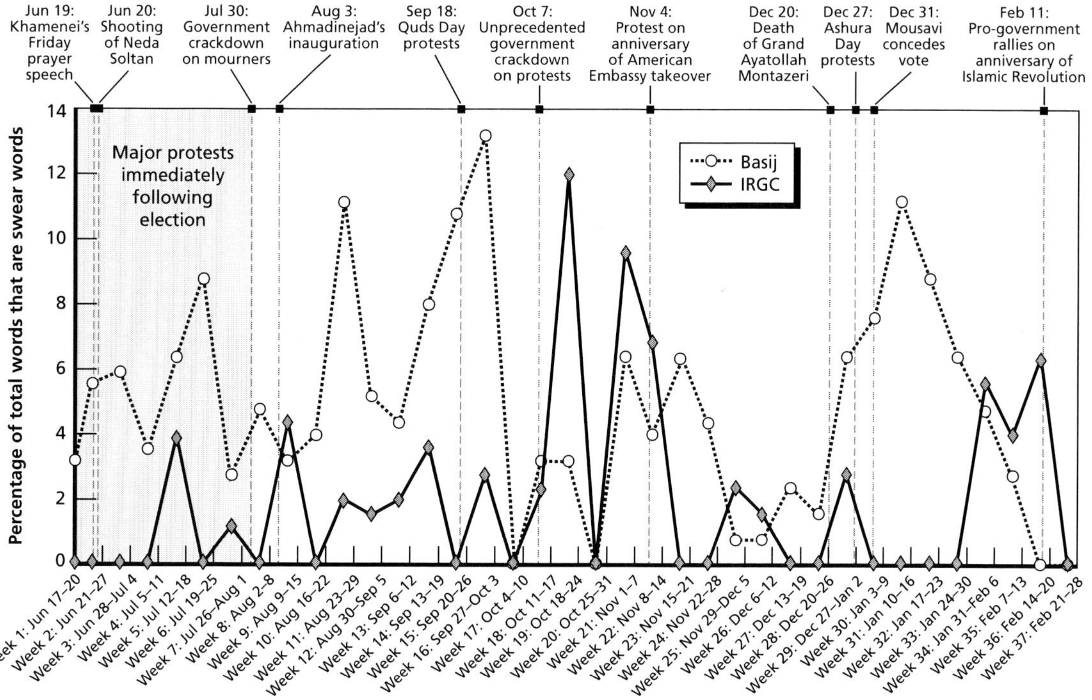

NOTES: The data points signify a ratio of the swear words to total words across an entire week's worth of tweets. Significant events in the aftermath of the election are noted at the top of the figure.
RAND *TR1161-5.8*

> retweetNew Video BASIJ PIGS SHOOTING INNOCENT PEOPLE BASIJ are FILTHY HEARTLESS ANIMALS. THEY'LL ROT IN HELL

> Shame on you Basij for torturing raping and killing innocent people. You and Khamenei will burn in hell

> a basij member isnt worth my time.hope he burns in hell for killing our neda!

Twitterers also swore at higher rates about the Basij than the IRGC in week 11 (August 23–29), suggesting another outburst of anger at them even though street protests had halted. This result parallels others presented in this report and suggests that even though no protests took place on the ground from late July to mid-September, people still felt angry at the Basij and wrote negatively about it. A review of the tweets from week 11 substantiates the idea that people swore about the Basij directly during this week. Swearing about the Basij increased during the week of the Quds Day protests (during week 14; September 13–19), reaching a crescendo at week 16 (September 27–October 3—before the government cracked down with increased intensity on the opposition). As with other results in this report, however, people reduced their swearing about the Basij by week 17 (October 4–10), coinciding with the intensified government crackdown.

Meanwhile, Twitterers began swearing at higher rates about the IRGC during week 19 (October 18–24). On October 18, at least five commanders of the IRGC had been killed in the restive southeast along Iran's frontier with Pakistan, according to Iranian state news agencies

(Slackman, 2009d). The strike on these commanders, one of the largest against the Guards in the region, appeared to mark an escalation in hostilities between Iran and the Baluchi ethnic minority. At this time, people tweeted about how several heads of state condemned the attack on the IRGC. An example of text that people retweeted many times is the following:

> It's Ironic that on a sunday morning four hours after atack on IRGC that heads of state incl USA2. condemn the attack.
>
> Where were they all on OCT 11 when the IRGC hung innocent Behnoud? It makes me wonder who's side the heads of state are on innocent civilians of Iran or the damn IRGC

Rates of swearing for both the Basij and the IRGC increased at week 21 (November 1–7), during the protests that took place on the anniversary of the takeover of the U.S. embassy (November 4). Interestingly, however, both rates decreased in the weeks before, during, and after the National Student Day protests on December 7. But swearing rates jumped again for the Basij during the week of the Ashura Day protests (December 27) and for the two weeks following it. In comparison, swearing rates for the IRGC stayed relatively low. As the opposition movement flagged, toward the end of the time period examined, swearing for both the Basij and the IRGC declined.

The fact that people swore increasingly about the Basij during the Quds Day and Ashura Day protests, among other findings, illustrates a use of the current methodology for intelligence analysts: assessing the impact of political actions on public opinion. In this case, people may have sworn at higher rates about the Basij during the Quds Day and Ashura Day protests because of the brutal way in which these forces cracked down on the protests. As such, studying the messages that Twitterers post can suggest to analysts how people may be reacting to events—even though it is not possible to prove a linkage between events and Twitter postings, per se.

The patterns in the way that Twitterers swore about both groups raise the question of why they might express more anger at the Basij. It is possible that Twitterers viewed the Basij as playing the most direct role in committing violence on the opposition. As noted above, opposition leader Mousavi decried the Basij for their lack of uniforms, identification, or anything that denotes them as public employees when they appeared with weapons. Although people did express anger toward the IRGC, the Basij appear to have loomed larger in their minds as having committed violence, torture, and rape. As one Twitterer put it:

> What is going on here? who are all these trolls where are the regulars?

Public Opinion About the United States, President Obama, and the CIA

Summary

- Especially early after the election, Twitter users expressed frustration with President Obama. There appeared to be a strong desire for Obama to make public statements in support of the Iranian protesters.
- Patterns of pronoun use that indicate a focus on others may suggest that people felt a greater sense of community when discussing President Obama, as opposed to when dis-

cussing Iranian public figures (i.e., Ahmadinejad, Khamenei, Karroubi, and Mousavi). They may also have felt more negatively about the Iranian leaders than they did about Obama.

- Trends in emotion-word usage show that people expressed more negative sentiment toward Supreme Leader Khamenei and President Ahmadinejad than toward President Obama throughout the period examined.
- Some Twitter users expressed suspicion that foreign entities—particularly intelligence agencies—had been attempting to influence the protests, and may have even been primary factors in the entire Green Movement.

This set of analyses focused on the United States and President Obama. We examined the words people used when writing about various topics associated with the United States. Specifically, we examined usage of the phrase "United States" and of its abbreviation (i.e., "U.S." or "U.S.A."[3]).[4] The other topics related to the United States included President Obama and the CIA.

For each of these topics, we concentrated on indicators that had revealed meaningful patterns in the overall view of public mood in Iran: swear words and pronouns. For each of these indicators, we (1) examined general trends over time and (2) compared changes (e.g., spikes) with actual political events regarding the United States. We also compared the patterns of these indicators for President Obama with those for the Iranian leaders (i.e., Ahmadinejad, Khamenei, Karroubi, and Mousavi).

Usage of Swear Words Suggests Early Frustration with the United States and President Obama, as Well as a Strong Desire for U.S. Action

Twitter users appeared to be intensely interested in the United States' stance on the Iranian presidential election. Particularly in the first few weeks after the election, elevated usage of curse words indicated considerable frustration at President Obama. As shown in Figure 5.9, during this period, people's usage of swear words when writing about the United States—and particularly, about President Obama—increased, peaking two weeks after the election. Initially, Obama offered relatively moderate comments about the election, careful not to be seen as "meddling" in Iran's affairs (BBC News, 2009b). During this time, swearing in tweets associated with him was accordingly at its highest point at any time in the approximately seven months following the election. Then, on June 23, President Obama appeared at a press confer-

---

[3] As discussed regarding methodology (see the appendix), "US" and "USA" are common letter combinations that may appear as part of other words unrelated to the United States. Therefore to capture usage of these references to the United States in the tweets, while eliminating unrelated usages, we only included letter combinations for "US" or "USA" that appeared at word boundaries. Specifically, we only included instances that were (1) surrounded by white space, (2) at the start/end of a line, or (3) after characters like '([-' with white space following them. To the extent possible, we also manually filtered out cases that appeared in phrases such as "GIVE US THE HELP..."

[4] Compared to usage of some variation of "US," "U.S." or "U.S.A.," usage of the more formal phrase "United States" was fairly minimal. Given the small sample size of available text, we dropped analysis of word usage related to "United States," focusing instead on patterns of the much more commonly used abbreviations. Throughout this section, however, we use the phrase "United States" for clarity, as opposed to referring to the abbreviated phrasings. Differences in the phrasings and wording choices used to refer to a topic may signal communication style (e.g., more or less formal), or may also indicate that different people are speaking. The implications of these different wording choices are discussed in the Methodological Considerations section. Other relevant phrasing differences discussed in that section include, for example, "Khamenei" and "Supreme Leader," and "IRGC" and "Revolutionary Guards."

Figure 5.9
Comparison of Swearing When Writing About the United States and Obama

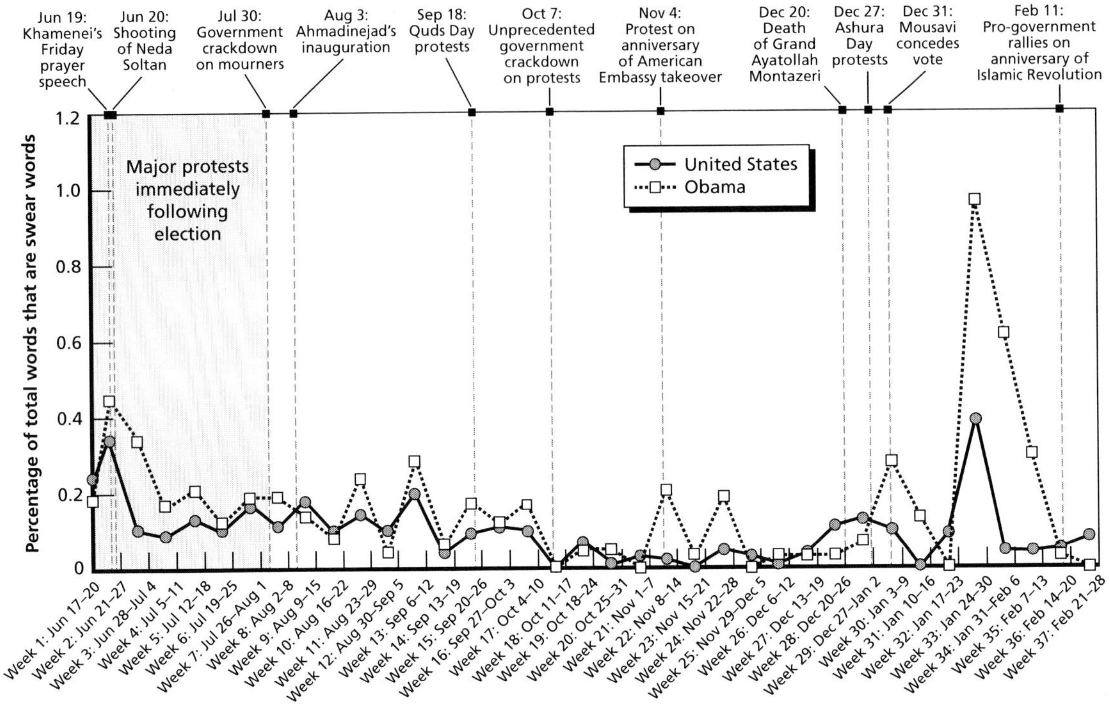

NOTES: The data points signify a ratio of the swear words to total words across an entire week's worth of tweets. Significant events in the aftermath of the election are noted at the top of the figure.
RAND *TR1161-5.9*

ence, strongly denouncing the violent crackdown against the protesters in Iran (Cooper and Sanger, 2009). Three days later, on June 26, he reinforced these comments, dismissing criticism from Iranian President Ahmadinejad of his earlier condemnations. At this time, Obama also explicitly distinguished Ahmadinejad from the leading opposition figure, Mousavi, who he hailed as an inspirational figure for the protesters (Zeleny, 2009). Coinciding with these statements of support for the protesters, swearing on Twitter regarding President Obama began to subside (e.g., June 28 to July 11).

An initial manual analysis of tweets from this two-week period reveals an active debate about the appropriate role of the United States and most useful actions (or inaction) that President Obama could undertake. On the one hand, some people, frustrated by the lack of a forceful U.S. response, wondered why President Obama "refused" to do anything to support the protest movement.

> obama - is this the strong leader he claims to be?

> why isnt obama talking about the speak up man!

Similarly, many tweets amounted to calls for action; people seemed anxious for President Obama to act (e.g., "obama is a chicken!" and "where is obama!"), generally by stating support for the protest.

But other Twitter users countered that Obama's moderation and relative silence were prudent, as they did not allow the Iranian regime any opportunity to blame the protests on foreign (i.e., U.S.) involvement or meddling.

> Obama wise to remove US as an excuse for Iran crackdown (and keep twitter up).
>
> from Iran: Obama cannot get involved Ahmadi must not have a reason to call this CIA revolt.
>
> from Iran: Obama doing fine. If he says anything in direct support of us government will say Evil US wants to destroy Iran
>
> I ask you americans. Please prevent your government from siding with reformists. It is going to backfire. Obama is right.

In considering what Twitter users were saying when discussing the Iran election, there was clearly keen awareness of U.S. foreign policy and in particular President Obama's public statements. For instance, a number of tweets from the weeks immediately following the election cited statements Obama made denouncing a coup against Honduran President Manuel Zelaya as illegal (BBC News, 2009c), wondering why he had not made a similar statement regarding Iran. These complaints echoed debates in mainstream media about his posture toward events in both countries.[5] More broadly, these individuals' suggestions and rhetorical questions posed to President Obama also echoed domestic political pressure for him to adopt a harder stance against the Iranian government (Wolfowitz, 2009; Landler, 2009).

Pressure from individuals on Twitter for Obama to support the protest movement—simply by denouncing government violence—is notable for its implication that people still perceive the U.S. presidency as a bully pulpit to provide moral leadership. The stated desire for action and words from President Obama may also be indicative of his personal popularity, or perhaps simply that people perceive him as influential.

After the initial spike, usage of swear words when writing about President Obama gradually declined to a relatively stable state for almost seven months, in fact dropping to zero at various points between October 2009 and January 2010. The 33rd week after the election (January 24–30), however, witnessed a huge spike in swear words associated with writing about Obama. This spike appears to primarily be due to people reporting news of Mohammad Javad Larijani (PressTV, 2010), secretary general of Iran's High Council for Human Rights, using a racial slur to refer to President Obama (Iran and Peykeiran, 2010):

> Javad Larijani uses racial slur in referring to Obama [retweeted many times]
>
> Larijani calls Obama "KaKa siah" It is almost like saying "nig" while Obama always talks about regime with respect

While this spike in swear words may not have been directed toward Obama, it nevertheless serves as an indicator of where a policy analyst should look more closely for information about what people think about Obama, and what events were occurring with regard to

[5] See, for example, the exchange posted on a blog hosted by *The Economist* ("Obama, Honduras, and Iran," 2009).

him. In this case, an analyst could see this spike, look more closely at tweets, and be able to get a sense that people were actually writing relatively positively about Obama. This spike in swear words may therefore be significant not only for its implications for policy, but also for its methodological implications. As we have suggested elsewhere, it may be particularly useful to bundle automated and manual content analysis techniques, such as by using the results from automated analysis to suggest topics or patterns deserving of closer manual attention.

Overall, the trend of swear-word usage related to President Obama was relatively similar to that for the United States, although the latter trend was generally flatter and less varying. There are a few possible conclusions to be drawn from this relationship. First, the topics are correlated—people simply wrote about both the country and its president at the same time. Second, the larger variations in writing styles around President Obama (e.g., higher spikes, more pronounced declines) may suggest that Twitter users felt more strongly about him than they did about the United States. Finally, it may be that individuals generally elicit stronger expressions of emotion than do nonhuman entities, such as nations.

While overall usage of swear words by the overall sample of Twitter users predicted events and protests, this was not necessarily so for swearing about a particular topic, such as the United States. In fact, it would seem logical that indicators (e.g., swear/curse words) associated with the United States are not predictive of Iranian protests, as the United States was not the main target of public anger or of the demonstrations themselves.

Results such as those concerning President Obama and the United States can inform outreach efforts to foreign populations, such as people within Iran. For example, the finding that Twitterers swore at relatively elevated rates about President Obama in the earliest weeks after the election and the specific analyses of what they wrote about him suggest that they wanted him to speak out in favor of the opposition. Such analyses can help the United States understand public opinion in Iran, given that the United States does not have an official presence there.

Usage of First-Person Singular Pronouns Regarding the United States and President Obama Generally Paralleled Usage of Swear Words

The patterns with which people used first-person singular pronouns when writing about the United States and President Obama were relatively similar to the patterns for swear words. Recall that usage of first-person singular pronouns (e.g., "I," "my") conveys feelings of depression. Taken together, usage of these pronouns as well as swear words suggest that Twitter users were debating the "proper" role for the United States in the Iranian protest movement.

As with swear words, the usage of these pronouns surrounding Obama is much more striking than is usage associated with the United States. Feelings of depression associated with Obama increased rapidly in the immediate aftermath of the election (see Figure 5.10), peaking around six weeks after the election (July 19–25).[6] Note, however, that this spike for first-person singular pronouns occurred slightly after the spike for swear words. This may suggest that initial frustration and anger eventually gave way to growing unease about the United States' stance on the election and possible courses of action.

---

[6] This increase in first-person singular pronouns does not necessarily indicate that people felt depressed or negative about Obama. Rather, their feelings should be examined in the larger context of the election. Given that the writing about Obama is actually a subset of writing about the Iran presidential election, interpretation of users' depressive feelings should be taken in the context of both the elections as well as Obama.

Figure 5.10
Usage of First-Person Singular Pronouns When Writing About the United States and Obama

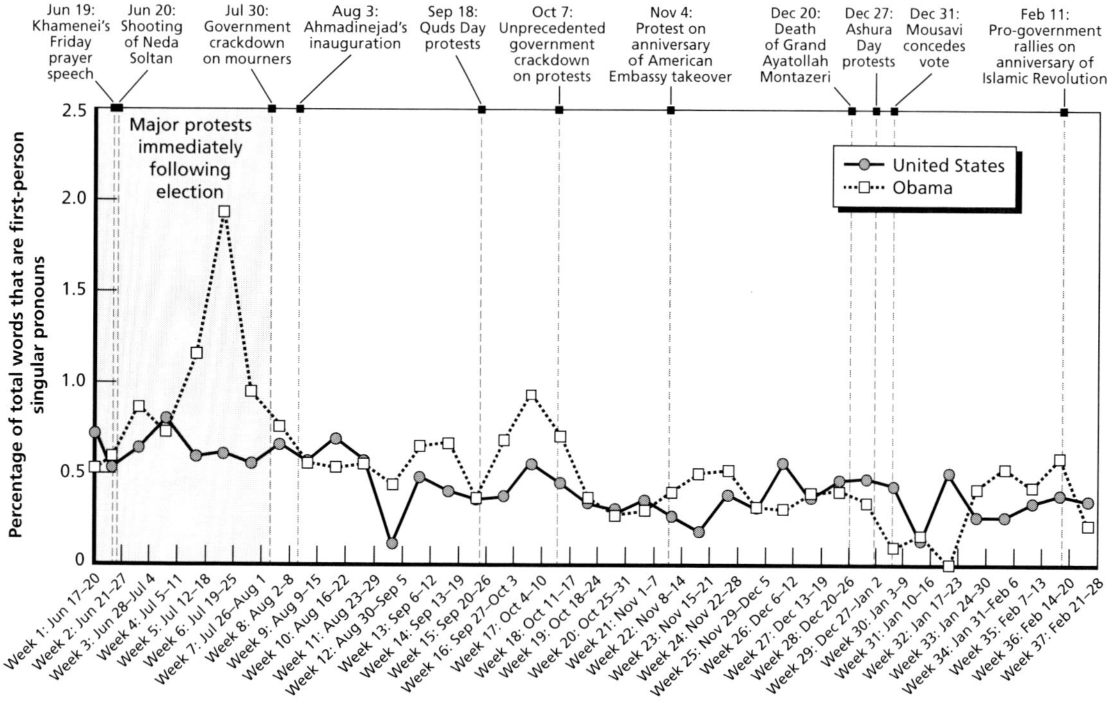

NOTES: The data points signify a ratio of the first-person singular pronouns to total words across an entire week's worth of tweets. Significant events in the aftermath of the election are noted at the top of the figure.
RAND *TR1161-5.10*

Manual analysis of the tweets related to President Obama suggests that this spike in first-person singular pronouns may have been due in large part to numerous variations of the following call for action: "Pres. Obama I respectfully request you not recognize the Ahmadinejad presidency."[7] Given how often this theme was repeated, the first-person singular pronoun indicator may suggest elevated insecurity at this time about Ahmadinejad and how legitimately the international community would perceive his rule.

After these first few weeks, first-person singular pronoun use generally declined until 34 weeks after election (January 31–February 6), where it again increased slightly. Interrupting the decline was a slight spike around the 17th week after the election (October 4–10).[8]

Manual analysis shows that tweets about President Obama during this week were dominated by discussion of his Nobel Peace Prize, which had been just announced on October 9. This dialogue about Obama's Nobel Prize occurred most often in the specific context of how it related to Iran. One particular point that Twitter users proudly noted was his reference, in his

---

[7] This tweet example is illustrative of the subtlety with which this methodology can analyze writing styles. While the sentiment expressed in the tweet appears relatively neutral, it is the wording choices that, in aggregate, reveal how people are feeling. The writer *chose* to use the word "I," rather than simply saying, for example, "Do not recognize the Ahmadinejad presidency." The overall changes in how such pronouns are used, rather than specific usages of them, are what suggest depressive states (or other attitudes and mood).

[8] This spike coincides with spikes in usage of first-person singular pronouns in tweets about Mousavi, Khamenei, and the Supreme Leader.

public statement about the award, to Neda Agha-Soltan. Overall, however, the spike in pronoun use appeared to reflect a fairly mixed set of positions on the implications of the award. For example,

> I have such mixed feelings about this obama winning thing. What has he concretely done yet besides great speeches iran: (

Many people clearly wanted to ensure that the significance of other events on the ground that week was not overlooked. These events include the death sentence for Mohammad Reza Ali Zamani and apparent funding cut for the U.S.-based Iran Human Rights Documentation Center, which had been preparing to investigate violence against Iranian protesters (Stockman, 2009).

Tweets using first-person singular pronouns but that did not refer specifically to the Nobel Prize expressed general displeasure with President Obama's perceived inaction toward or lack of support for the Iranian protest movement.

> Just reflecting im really really shocked that USA government/Obama has literally tried to silence and ignore protest!

> I wrote Obama a letter today asking him to explain his non-actions on humanrights. Join me?

> I wonder what all the Obama supporters make of the fact that he stopt funding Iran HRA. Is this the "change" he talked about?

During this period, first-person singular pronoun usage associated with the United States was at its highest level than at any other time in the nine months following the Iranian election, though not as high as the spike in first-person singular pronoun usage associated with President Obama. In other words, the trend for first-person singular pronouns when writing about the United States, while generally tracking the trend for Obama, appears relatively less sensitive to change. In particular, it did not show the sharp spike in depressive feelings following the election as with Obama. There was, however, elevated usage of first-person singular pronouns immediately after the election, and a similarly gradual decline before a slight increase, matching a slight increase for Obama.

Pronoun Use When Writing About Obama as Compared with Iranian Figures

Certain intriguing patterns emerged when comparing the ways that people used pronouns when discussing President Obama with the ways they used pronouns when discussing major Iranian figures (i.e., Ahmadinejad, Khamenei, Karroubi, and Mousavi). Recall that the use of first-person plural, second-person singular and plural, and third-person singular and plural pronouns implies a focus on interacting with others. Across these "other-focused" pronouns, usage was higher than or at least comparable when people wrote about Obama versus when they wrote about the Iranian leaders. This may suggest that people felt more connected and more of a collective identity when speaking about President Obama.

To illustrate these relationships, we present comparisons of first-person plural pronoun usage when writing about Obama and Ahmadinejad (Figure 5.11) and Obama and Mousavi

Figure 5.11
Usage of First-Person Plural Pronouns When Writing About Obama and Ahmadinejad

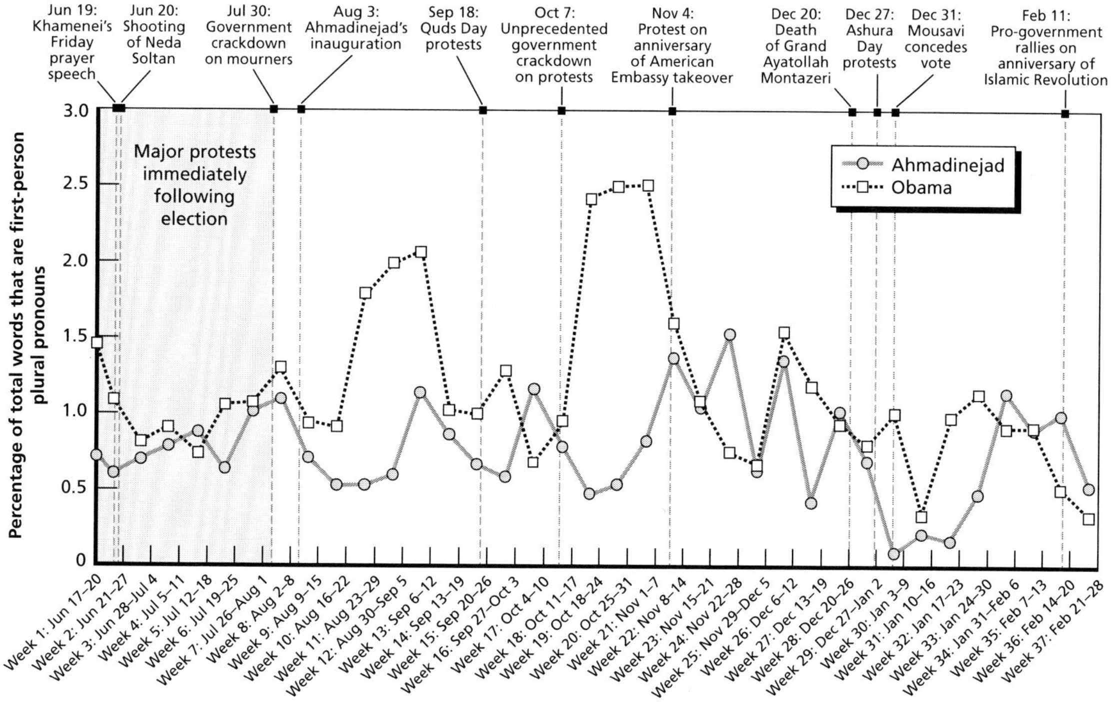

NOTES: The data points signify a ratio of the first-person plural pronouns to total words across an entire week's worth of tweets. Significant events in the aftermath of the election are noted at the top of the figure.
RAND *TR1161-5.11*

(Figure 5.12). In both cases, the trend line for Obama is higher, for most of the nine months, than that for either Ahmadinejad or Mousavi.

Conversely, usage of self-focused pronouns (i.e., first-person singular pronouns) when writing about Obama was comparable to or slightly lower than usage when writing about the Iranian figures.[9] Figures 5.13 and 5.14 show usage of first-person singular pronouns when writing about Obama and Ahmadinejad, and Obama and Mousavi, respectively. With the exception of an early spike for Obama in both cases, the trend in first-person singular pronoun usage is generally lower for Obama than for either Ahmadinejad or Mousavi. This may suggest that people felt more negative and uncertain regarding the Iranian leaders than they did about President Obama.

On one level, this finding makes intuitive sense, given that the Iranian leaders should be more closely identified with the presumably traumatic fallout of the disputed election. This finding may further suggest that usage of self-focused pronouns may in fact constitute a sort of inverse "approval rating" that may complement traditional opinion polling. In other words, comparisons between public figures using this indicator may be able to suggest their *unpopularity* relative to each other. Future research may seek to validate this indicator as such.

---

[9] One exception was the initial elevated level and spike in feelings of depression and frustration surrounding President Obama in the weeks immediately following the election. This meant that usage of first-person singular pronouns was higher when people wrote about Obama than when they wrote about the Iranian political figures at that time.

Figure 5.12
Usage of First-Person Plural Pronouns When Writing About Obama and Mousavi

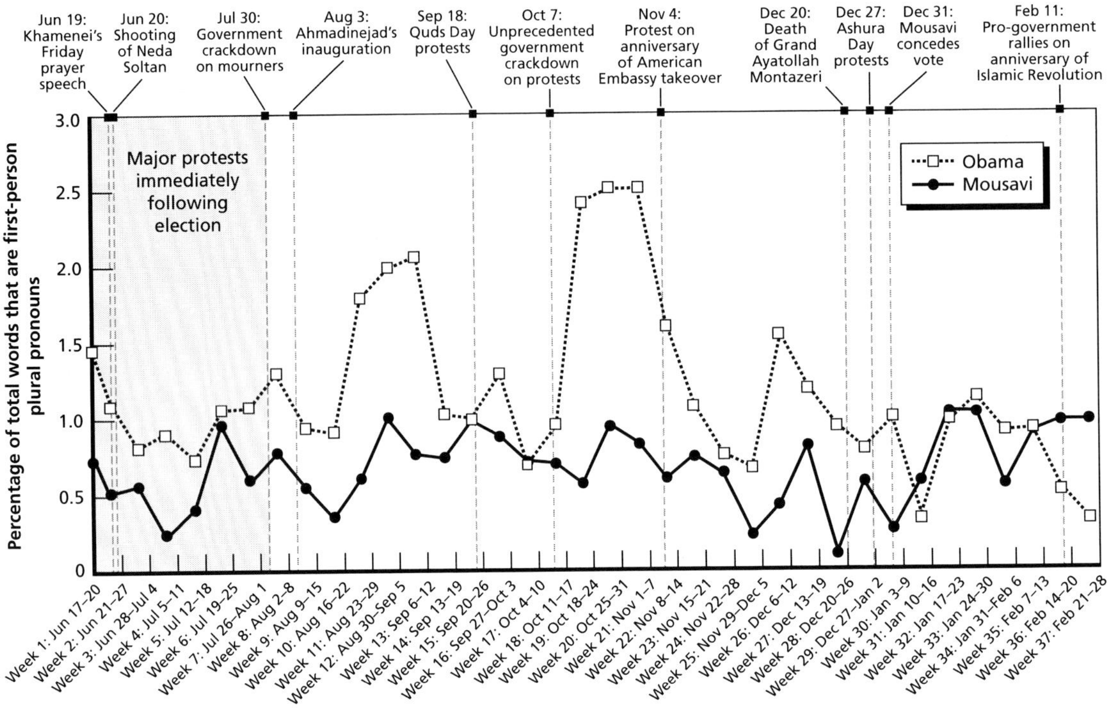

NOTES: The data points signify a ratio of the first-person plural pronouns to total words across an entire week's worth of tweets. Significant events in the aftermath of the election are noted at the top of the figure.
RAND *TR1161-5.12*

Twitter Users Expressed Less Negative Emotion When Writing About Obama as Compared with Iranian Figures

We also compared Twitterers' emotional expressions regarding President Obama and Iranian political leaders. We found similar results across two indicators.

Specifically, we examined the trends for the "sadness" indicator and the "anxiety" indicator. In both cases, a manual inspection of the tweets shows that Twitter users expressed negative sentiment toward the Iranian government leaders but not necessarily sadness or anxiety per se. Figure 5.15 shows the trend lines for Supreme Leader Khamenei, President Ahmadinejad, and President Obama according to the "sadness" indicator. As the figure shows, Twitter users expressed more negative sentiment toward Supreme Leader Khamenei and President Ahmadinejad than toward President Obama throughout the entire time period examined. Some examples of tweets regarding Supreme Leader Khamenei (taken from weeks 27 and 28, corresponding to December 13–26) are the following:

> Khamenei stares failure in the face: no dynasty other than disgrace

> When stmnt of SL read mournrs jumped up and down booing and screamng "Khamenei is a murderer. His leadership is finished"

> Mourners chanted against Khamenei Ahmadinejad and Basij and demanded release of prisoners

Figure 5.13
Usage of First-Person Singular Pronouns When Writing About Obama and Ahmadinejad

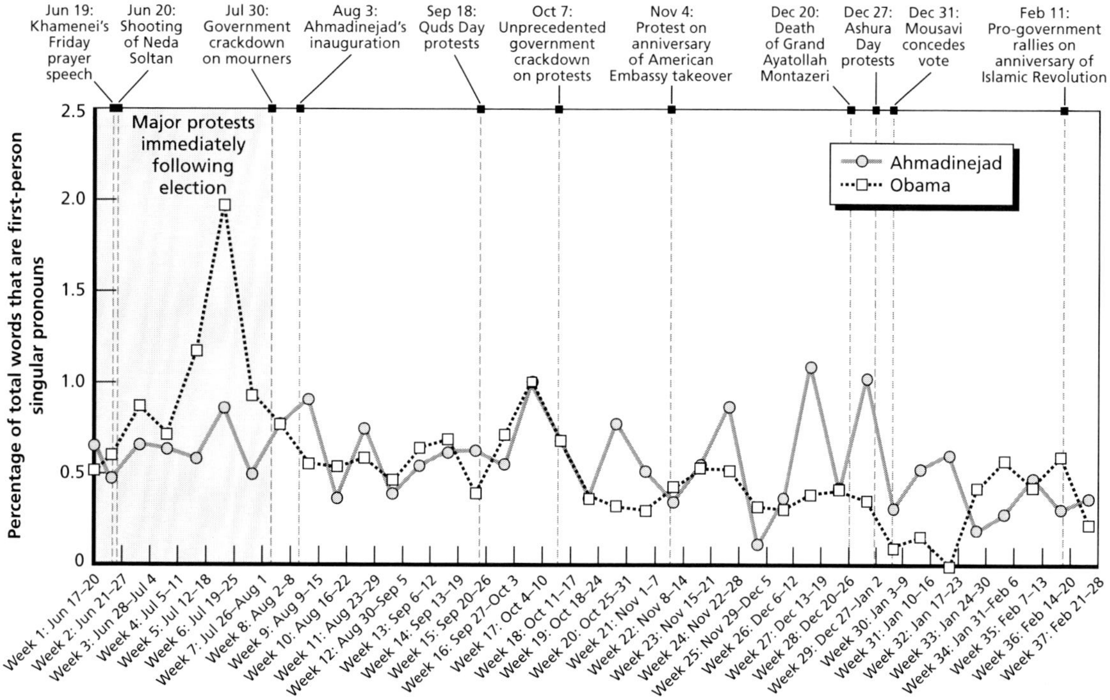

NOTES: The data points signify a ratio of the first-person singular pronouns to total words across an entire week's worth of tweets. Significant events in the aftermath of the election are noted at the top of the figure.
RAND *TR1161-5.13*

Another indicator of sentiment expressed toward President Obama and Iranian government leaders is that of "anxiety." Once again, the "anxiety" indicator did not necessarily capture expressions of anxiety, per se, but more generalized negative expressions toward Supreme Leader Khamenei and President Ahmadinejad, as compared with President Obama. Figure 5.16 demonstrates these trends in the indicator. As the figure shows, Twitterers expressed substantially higher amounts of negative sentiment toward Supreme Leader Khamenei and President Ahmadinejad than toward President Obama throughout the entire time period examined. Examples of tweets regarding Supreme Leader Khamenei from weeks 28 and 29 (corresponding to December 20–January 2) illustrate these expressions:

> Yazid Scared!
>
> Huge number of security and special forces seen protecting Khamenei Residence.
>
> Shame that Montazeri did not become SL after Khomeini. Instead Iran got supreme megalomaniac Khamenei Also remb - Khamenei wasn't even an Ayatollah before he became Supreme Lead
>
> Khamenei is the biggest sponsor of terrorism throughout the middle-east and that turban-headed terrorist must be dealt with

Figure 5.14
Usage of First-Person Singular Pronouns When Writing About Obama and Mousavi

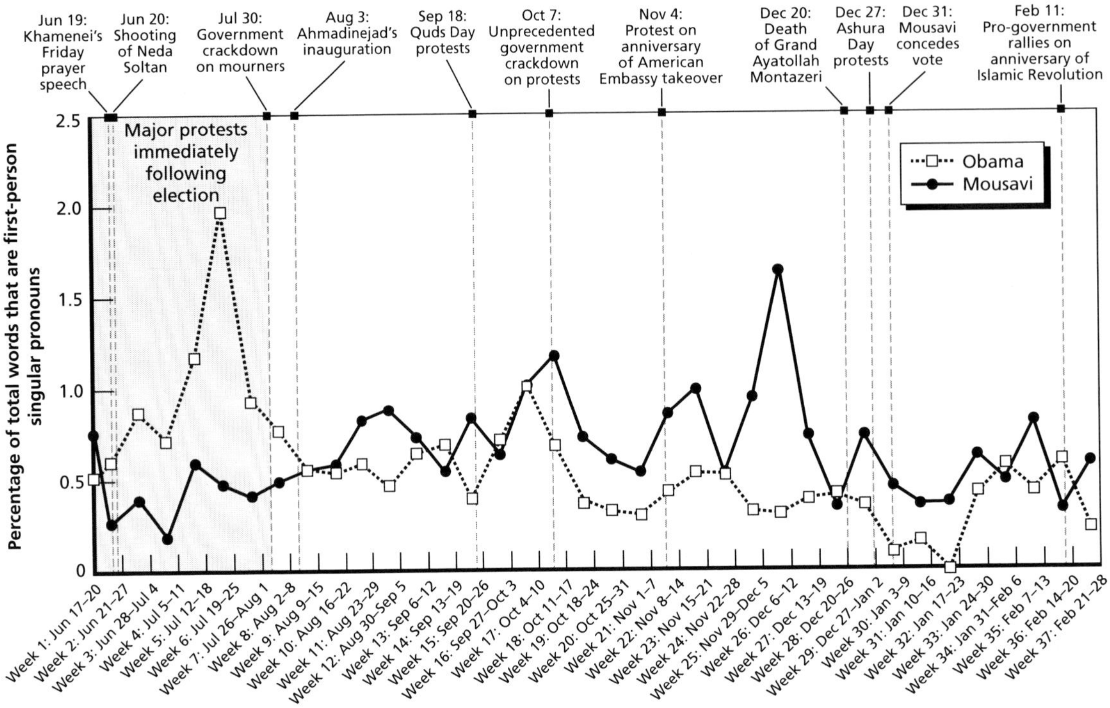

NOTES: The data points signify a ratio of the first-person singular pronouns to total words across an entire week's worth of tweets. Significant events in the aftermath of the election are noted at the top of the figure.
RAND *TR1161-5.14*

The fact that Twitter users wrote substantially more negatively about Supreme Leader Khamenei and President Ahmadinejad than about President Obama illustrates a use of this methodology for intelligence analysts: to make informed assessments of public opinion in countries like Iran. Although one might have inferred from events on the ground that people felt angry at Supreme Leader Khamenei and President Ahmadinejad, only methodologies such as presented in this project can shed light on comparative differences between how people felt about both Iranian leaders and President Obama. More conventional surveys, for example, would encounter the problem that people cannot speak freely in Iran's current political climate.

Positive Emotions in Tweets About Obama Showed Several Pronounced Spikes Compared with Tweets About the United States

As with the other indicators (pronouns and swear words), usage of positive-emotion words when people wrote about Obama seemed to be much more sensitive to political events compared with when they wrote about the United States. Figure 5.17 shows that usage of positive-emotion words was fairly similar regarding the United States and Obama, with the prominent exception of several large spikes regarding Obama. The first of these spikes came in the week immediately following Ahmadinejad's inauguration (August 9–15). Also, this spike in positive emotion regarding Obama occurred just a few weeks after feelings of depression (i.e., usage of first-person singular pronouns) when writing about him had spiked.

A second, larger spike in usage of positive-emotion words came at the 17th week after the election (October 4–10), when President Obama was awarded the Nobel Peace Prize. This fits

Figure 5.15
Comparison of Sadness Words When Writing About Obama, Khamenei, and Ahmadinejad

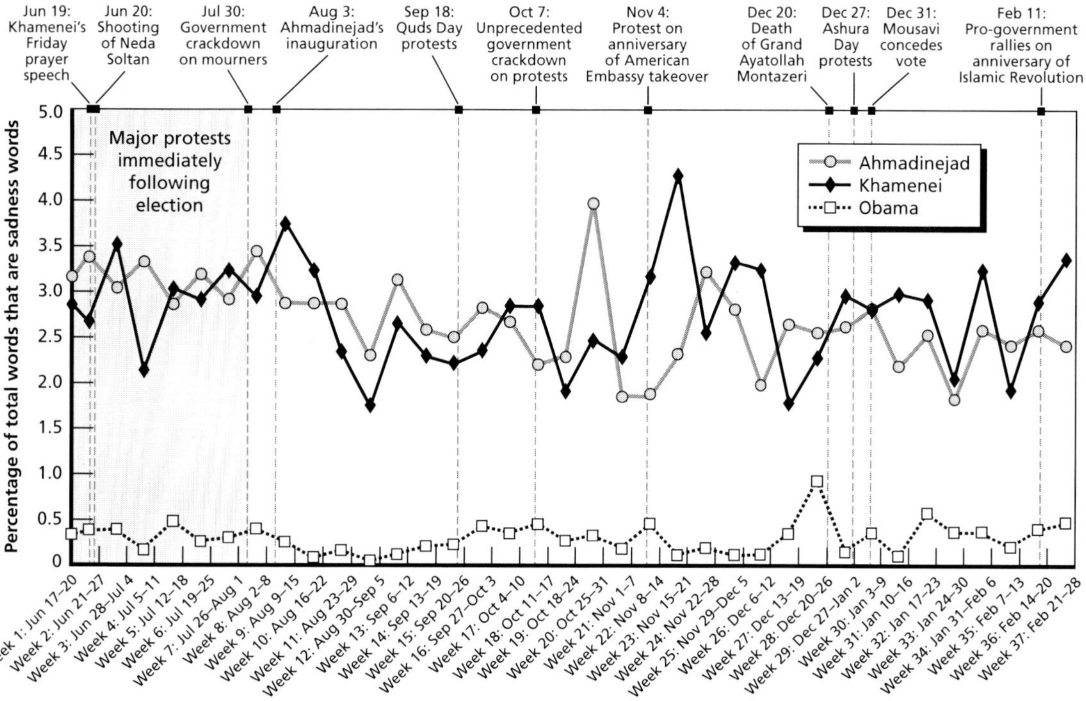

NOTES: The data points signify a ratio of sadness words to total words across an entire week's worth of tweets. Significant events in the aftermath of the election are noted at the top of the figure.
RAND *TR1161-5.15*

with the manual analysis of tweets (described above) showing mixed feelings—but including pride and other positive emotions—expressed about the award. Finally, there was a spike in positive emotions at the 32nd week after the election (January 17–23), the week before news of Larijani referring to Obama using a racial slur.

Some Twitter Users Pointed to Foreign Influence, Particularly Intelligence Agencies, as the Driving Force Behind Protests

Throughout recent history, it has been argued, Iranians have believed that the United States possessed both the capacity and desire to effect political change in Iran (Pollack, 2004). Comments and speculation over Twitter (albeit from a small sample of messages) regarding foreign influence in the Green Movement and protests appear to support this view.

We conducted initial manual analyses of tweets referring to "CIA."[10] Mentions of the CIA generally appeared to refer to its supposed role in Iranian affairs, perhaps even as behind the Green Movement. Also of note was the fact that people referred frequently to other intelligence agencies (e.g., "FBI," "MI6") in conjunction with the CIA, as possibly working together.

> Naif to think CIA or Mossad s not supporting Armed Resistance in Iran. Its common thing. And maby we need some little help

[10] While people referred repeatedly to the CIA and to other foreign government agencies, the actual number of references did not comprise a large enough sample with which to run LIWC analysis.

Figure 5.16
Comparison of Anxiety When Writing About Obama, Khamenei, and Ahmadinejad

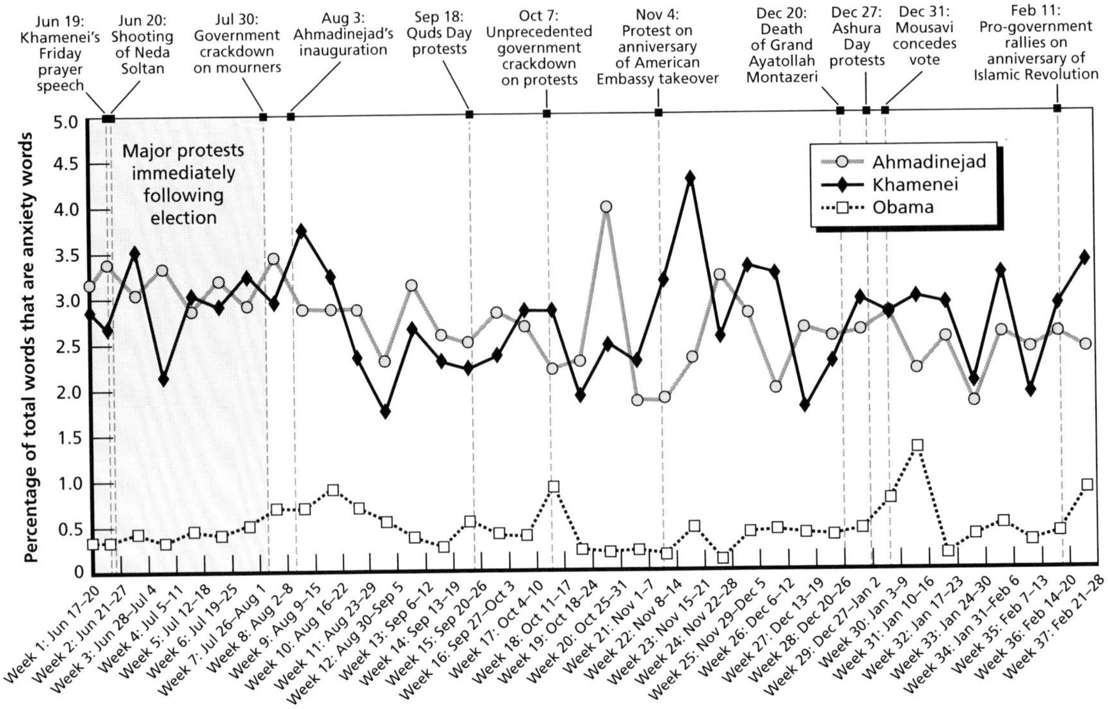

NOTES: The data points signify a ratio of anxiety words to total words across an entire week's worth of tweets. Significant events in the aftermath of the election are noted at the top of the figure.
RAND *TR1161-5.16*

> I hope every1 is aware that Iran's Intel Service isn't the only1 trying to influence CIA MI6 etc. are here too.

Nor were Twitter users the only source of such speculation; public figures within the Iranian government also implicated foreign actors. President Ahmadinejad pronounced the opposition movement to be "a Zionist and American ordered masquerade" (Haaretz Service and the Associated Press, 2009). In a televised New Year speech, Khameini referred to U.S. government efforts to "plot and plan sedition" (BBC News, 2010c). Accordingly, there were rumors that during this time government plants lurked on Twitter and other social media, attempting to either influence others or pinpoint dissidents. This possibility would seem plausible in light of tweets such as this:

> Keep in mind that CIA Mossad and others are in favor of chaos and unrest in Iran. Separatism is what they would like to see.

Due to the small number of tweets in this sample that mentioned foreign agencies, and accusations by the Iranian government of foreign influence, it is unclear whether these tweets represent either opposition movement or pro-regime viewpoints, or even efforts of the rumored government plants. Indeed, it would be ironic that people related to the Green Movement, characterized as "bottom-up" and "grassroots" ("Iranian Protest Is Grassroots and Unstoppable, Say Activists, 2009") and communicating over a decentralized network such as Twitter, might yet see an unseen hand shaping their protests. The implied persistence of such atti-

Figure 5.17
Usage of Positive-Emotion Words When Writing About the United States and Obama

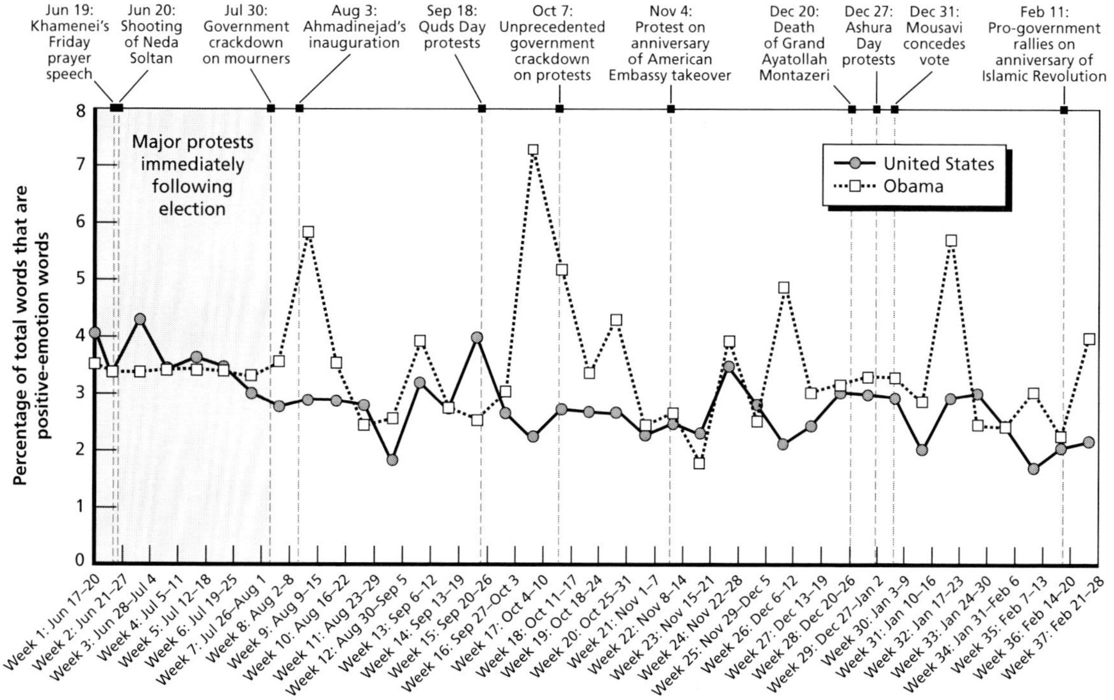

NOTES: The data points signify a ratio of positive-emotion words to total words across an entire week's worth of tweets. Significant events in the aftermath of the election are noted at the top of the figure.
RAND *TR1161-5.17*

tudes may suggest that policymakers seeking to issue public statements or take other actions regarding foreign political movements should consider even more carefully the impact of those actions on the perceptions of foreign populations.

Public Opinion About Specific Countries: Israel, the United States, and Iran

Summary

- Twitterers expressed little negative sentiment toward Israel or the United States. This suggests that Twitterers did not focus their anger on Iran's traditional enemies in the aftermath of the election.
- Twitterers expressed little negative sentiment toward "Iran" but considerable anger toward the "Islamic Republic." This suggests that the focus of their anger was not the country of Iran, but rather the government that rules it.

We analyzed the tweets for clues as to how Twitterers felt about specific countries, such as Israel. Tensions have run high between Iran and Israel in light of President Ahmadinejad's comments that Israel should be "wiped off the map" (BBC News, "Iran Leader's Comments Attacked," October 27, 2005) and the potential threat of Israel bombing Iran's nuclear sites (Applebaum, 2010). Given these tensions, we examined what Twitter users wrote about Israel after the disputed election in Iran. Furthermore, to place Twitterers' writings about Israel in perspective, we compared the tone of their tweets with that of tweets about Iran itself and about the United States. Because Twitterers' tendency to swear about certain topics has served as the most valid indicator of how they feel, we examined the extent to which they used these words about all three countries.

Twitter Users Only Infrequently Swore Regarding Israel or the United States

An initial inspection of the tweets containing swear words and the word "Israel" suggests that people felt relatively little anger toward that country. Swearing was infrequent throughout the time period examined except during the first week (June 17–20) and the 25th week (November 29–December 5). At both points in time, it turned out that most Twitterers whose tweets about Israel contained swear words were not swearing about Israel per se. One topic of discussion during the first week, for example, consisted of Twitterer(s) in the West swearing at people inside Iran because they "hate both Israel and the USA." Then, during the 25th week (November 29–December 5), Twitterers quoted President Ahmadinejad as saying that Israel could not do a thing to stop Iran's nuclear activities. But Twitterers appeared to rarely swear directly about Israel.

Likewise, Twitterers tended not to swear directly about the United States. Swearing about the "USA" also stayed relatively low throughout the period examined except for two spikes, one at week 2 (June 21–27) and one at week 25 (November 29–December 5). An initial inspection of the tweets during week 2 shows that the following tweet was retweeted many times:

> 99% of tweets are from US backing a BLOODY revolution. People are dying. STOP destabilizing the Iranian state!

Although this tweet could have been posted by someone in the opposition movement, it seems more plausible that a government supporter posted this tweet in order to discredit the opposition movement, and then the tweet was re-posted many times. In that sense, the spike in negativity toward the "USA" in week 2 is probably a spurious one. Because retweets implicitly reflect an individual's attitudes and opinions, they should not be considered inherently detrimental to analyses of public opinion and mood. This spike, however, suggests that they may be used to efficiently flood the public discourse on a given topic, which would likely obscure true public opinion as measured by LIWC indicators. Manual analysis, however, should be able to identify such occurrences. Regarding the spike that occurred in week 25, one of the most common tweets during that week containing a swear word consisted of a quote of Javad Larijani, who used an obscenity to refer to President Obama. As described earlier, Twitter users who quoted Larijani on Twitter and discussed what he said tended to take a more positive view of President Obama. In that sense, once again, the spike in negativity for "USA" during week 25 was a spurious one.[11]

---

[11] We also examined the more formal phrase "United States," but found almost no swear words used in conjunction with this phrase throughout the entire period examined. Because of text length constraints, acronyms such as "U.S." or "USA" are likely preferred to the phrase "United States."

Twitter Users Swore More When Referring to the "Islamic Republic" Than to "Iran"

Finally, we examined how Twitterers wrote about Iran itself. We did this in two ways: first, by examining the tweets that contain "Iran," and second, by examining tweets that contain the "Islamic Republic." We did this because the two phrases are slightly different ways of referring to Iran: The word "Iran" simply denotes the country itself, while the phrase "Islamic Republic" connotes the type of country Iran became in 1979 after conservative clerical forces established a theocratic system of government. Without knowing which phrase might be the "better" one to examine, we analyzed both.

Twitter users wrote in drastically different ways depending on their phrasing. When using the phrase "Iran," they used relatively few swear words, and an initial inspection of the tweets suggests that people were not swearing about Iran directly. However, when Twitterers wrote about the "Islamic Republic," they significantly increased their use of swear words and directed these specifically at the "Islamic Republic" (see Figure 5.18).

As Figure 5.18 shows, swearing about the Islamic Republic peaked in the first week after the election and spiked at many points throughout the time period examined, such as the Quds Day protests (September 18), the protests on the anniversary of the takeover of the U.S. embassy (November 4), and the Ashura protests (December 27). An initial inspection of the tweets from each spike suggests that people referred directly to the Islamic Republic when they swore. After the Ashura protests, however, swearing about the Islamic Republic on aver-

Figure 5.18
Comparison of Swear Words When Writing About the "Islamic Republic" and "Iran" After the 2009 Election

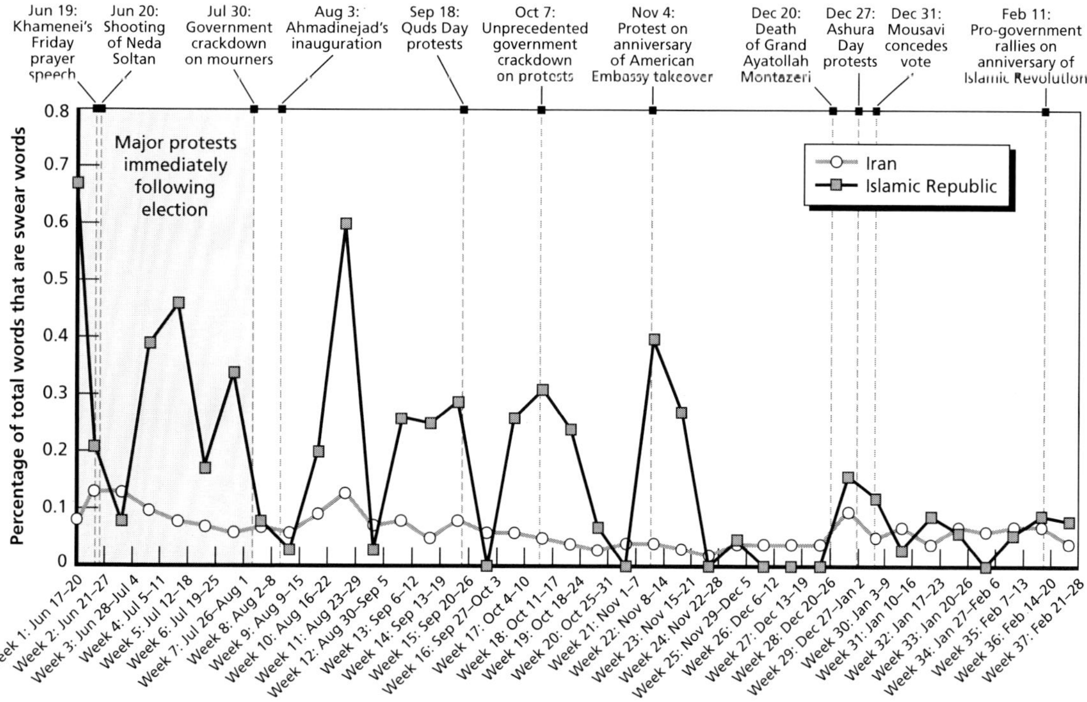

NOTES: The data points signify a ratio of swear words to total words across an entire week's worth of tweets. Significant events in the aftermath of the election are noted at the top of the figure.

RAND *TR1161-5.18*

age declined, paralleling other results and suggesting that anger died down as the opposition movement itself waned.

Overall, these results suggest that people using the IranElection hashtag on Twitter after the election felt a significant amount of anger toward the "Islamic Republic"—that is, toward the government that took power in 1979 and rules Iran. But they expressed little, if any, anger toward Israel, the United States, or "Iran" itself. When comparing the "Islamic Republic" and "Iran," it is possible that people vented more anger at the "Islamic Republic" because they associate it with the government in power, while "Iran" is simply a country with which they have other associations. Some examples of this distinction people may have drawn are the tweets below:

> Our common goal right now is to FREE IRAN from the bloody repressive Islamic Republic

> Important to educate people to rally for a common cause: the destruction of the bloody Islamic regime.[12]

Twitter Users Expressed Positive Emotions Toward Israelis Who May Have Aided the Protest Movement

A large spike in positive emotions regarding Israel in week 26 (December 6–12, see Figure 5.19) suggests that this indicator accurately expressed how Twitter users felt about Israel. In particular, a manual inspection of the tweets in this period reveals that Twitter users were in fact writing positively about people in Israel who appeared to be supporting the protest movement:

> Israel left parties Do your parthelp propagate PEACE. FREE IRAN is already doing it

While it is unclear what specific actions these Israelis had undertaken, it is notable for the implication of communications between Israelis and Iranians, and for the implied sympathies of at least some people in Israel.

As with other findings presented in this report, the findings regarding how people wrote about Israel, the United States, "Iran," and the "Islamic Republic" illustrate the potential for the current methodology to help analysts make informed assessments of public opinion in countries such as Iran.

---

[12] As noted in the appendix, in certain cases, we used a keyword stem (in this case, "Islamic") to capture additional variations, and thus more usages, of those keywords (in this case, "Islamic Republic"). We also inspected the tweets themselves to verify that the stems captured the appropriate tweets.

Figure 5.19
Usage of Positive-Emotion Words When Writing About Israel After the 2009 Election

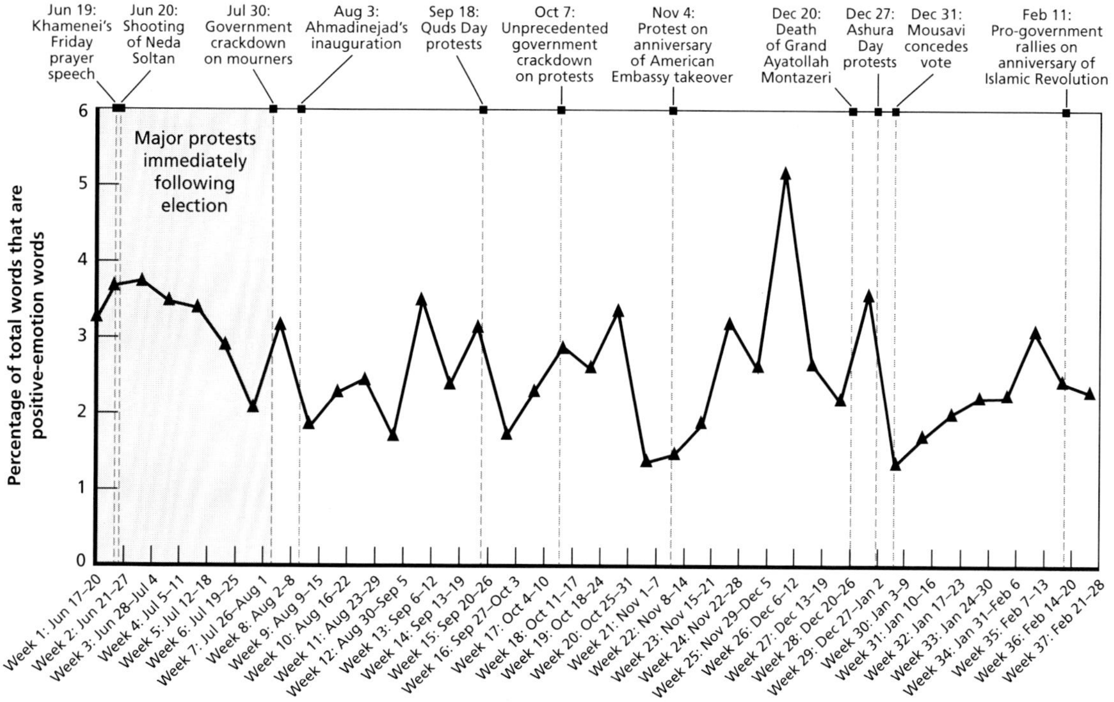

NOTES: The data points signify a ratio of positive-emotion words to total words across an entire week's worth of tweets. Significant events in the aftermath of the election are noted at the top of the figure.
RAND *TR1161-5.19*

Methodological Considerations

In addition to indicating trends in Iranian public opinion, our results revealed important methodological considerations and limitations. These issues may inform how policymakers apply this methodology to future uses.

Additional Demonstration of the Methodology: Sadness Words

In analyzing the IranElection tweets, we discovered one linguistic indicator—sadness—that also yielded results appearing to validate the methodology. Twitterers' use of "sadness" words spiked at two points in time that fit well with events on the ground (see Figure 6.1). First,

Figure 6.1
Patterns in Sadness Expressed on Twitter After the Election

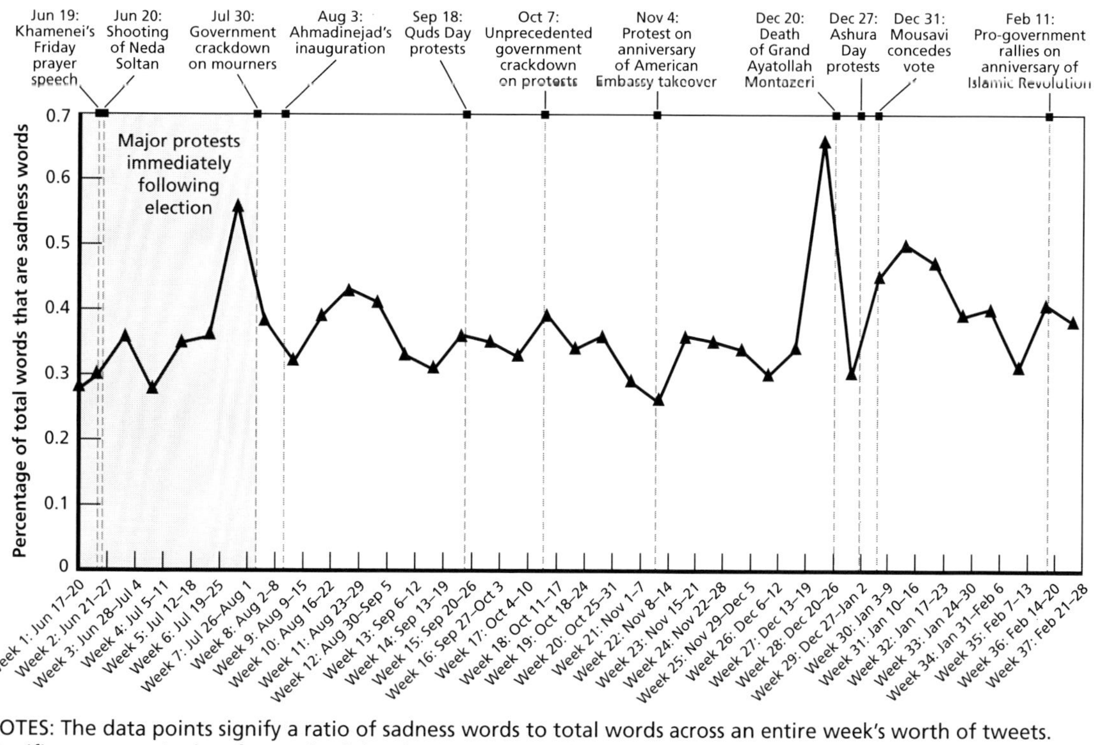

NOTES: The data points signify a ratio of sadness words to total words across an entire week's worth of tweets. Significant events in the aftermath of the election are noted at the top of the figure.

RAND *TR1161-6.1*

sadness words spiked during the week that included the 40th day after the death of Neda Soltan (i.e., week 7 after the election, or July 26–August 1; the 40th day after Neda's death was July 30). Fortieth-day observances honoring the dead are common in the Middle East and stem from a tradition of commemorating the burial of the Imam Hussein 40 days after Ashura (Ayoub, 1986). In the days leading up to and including July 30, use of the word "mourn" spiked as Twitterers wrote about the efforts of Mousavi, Karroubi, and Neda's mother to organize a ceremony to mourn Neda's death as well as the deaths of other protesters.

The second major spike in sadness words occurred on the day that influential dissident cleric Grand Ayatollah Hossein Ali Montazeri died, according to an analysis of word usage by day. Because we would have expected increased sadness at both points in time, these results serve to validate the sadness indicator and this methodological approach in general. One might wonder why sadness did not spike when Neda herself died (in week 1 of our chart). A possible explanation is that Neda did not become a known figure until after she died, when Iranians broadcast images of her death all over the world.

Linguistic Indicators That Did Not Work as Expected on Twitter

Although several indicators of emotional states and social processes expressed through Twitter yielded results that made intuitive sense, some indicators did not work as expected. In particular, when we examined ways that Twitterers wrote about certain leaders, some indicators identified a general emotion that Twitterers felt but not one that they associated specifically with the leader. These indicators warrant discussion, as well as a caution to those seeking to use automated approaches to text analysis—especially when trying to understand how people feel about specific leaders or topics. Potential users of this methodology should understand that each of the indicators, as currently constructed, is a composite set of many words. In fact, because the current indicators each include so many words, some of them yielded correct interpretations in the cases we examined (based on manual examination of tweets) but incorrect interpretations in others. Three such potentially misleading indicators are sadness, positive emotion, and anxiety. We encountered problems with these three in this research, but this does not mean that problems would only occur with these indicators. Rather, the results described in this section suggest that one should test any indicator for validity before using it and should continue to run spot-checks.

The sadness indicator correctly identified sadness at times when people mourned the deaths of prominent figures, but it did not always show that Twitterers associated sadness with specific leaders. For example, Figure 6.2 suggests that Twitterers wrote with sadness about Karroubi in the initial weeks after the election. However, a manual inspection of the tweets suggests that this is not the case, and that Twitterers wrote instead about Karroubi's efforts to coordinate a mourning ceremony for protestors who had died.

Concerning the positive-emotion indicator, our analysis above showed that it correctly pinpointed Twitterers' positive sentiment toward Karroubi after the Quds Day protests. However, it also indicated more positive emotion toward Ahmadinejad than toward Mousavi in the initial weeks after the election (see Figure 6.3). According to a follow-up automated analysis, the most common positive-emotion words that Twitterers used when writing about Ahmadinejad were "support," "please," and "like." In a manual sample of tweets we collected containing these words, most Twitterers who used them actually said something negative about Ahmadinejad,

Figure 6.2
Seeming Patterns in Sadness Expressed When Writing About Karroubi and Mousavi

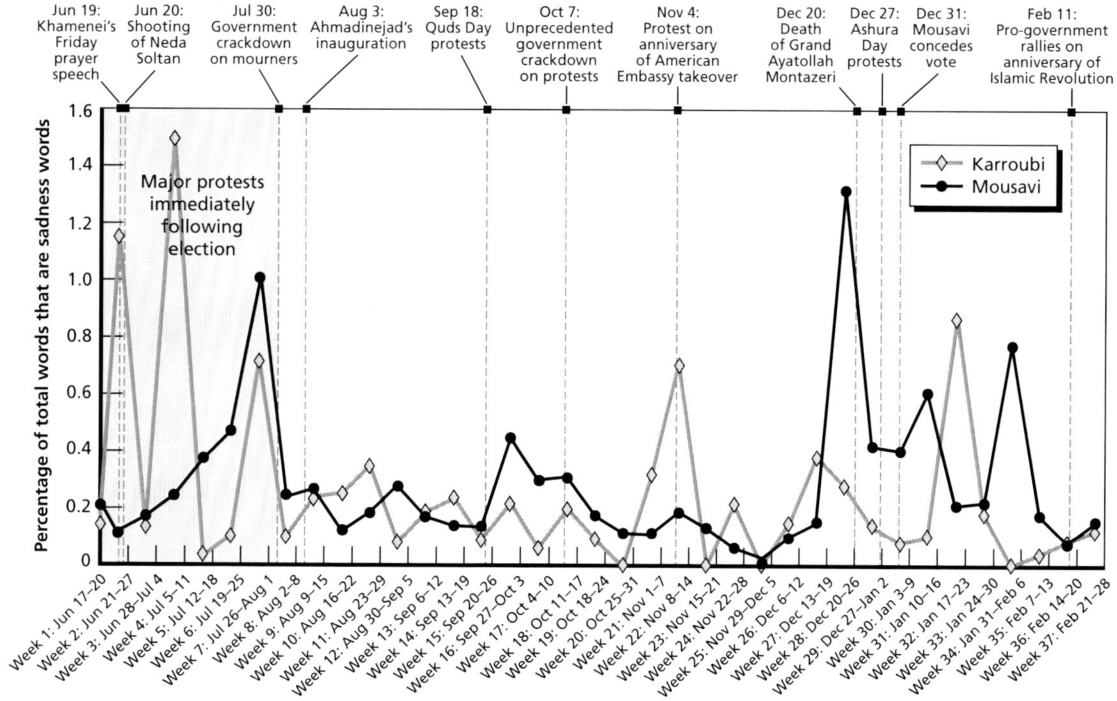

NOTES: The data points signify a ratio of sadness words to total words across an entire week's worth of tweets. Significant events in the aftermath of the election are noted at the top of the figure.
RAND *TR1161-6.2*

such as "shame to russia for supporting ahmadinajid your election is similar to iran..." The positive-emotion indicator was therefore misleading in appearing to have identified a sense of positive emotion associated with Ahmadinejad.

Finally, as discussed above, our indicator of anxiety includes the words "shame" and "ashamed," which Twitterers used in reference to Khamenei more than to Ahmadinejad in the days surrounding the Quds Day protests. Although the indicator accurately captured negative sentiment in that case, it did not function the same way in another case. Figure 6.4 shows that Twitterers used the word "ashamed" in connection with Karroubi more so than with Mousavi at several points throughout the nine-month period. However, they used this word most often when quoting Karroubi as saying he felt ashamed that the government would spread lies about the security forces (during week 6, or July 19–25) when the security forces claimed some of their own had been martyred. In this case, Twitterers were not writing with "shame" or anxiety about Karroubi. As with positive emotion, the anxiety indicator was misleading in appearing to reflect sentiment expressed in reference to Karroubi.

Differences in Phrasing May Reflect Differing Intentions and Writing Styles

How people refer to various topics when writing over social media may affect how those topics are analyzed. Any language may have several ways of referring to the same thing, whether an

Figure 6.3
Seeming Patterns in Positive Emotion Expressed When Writing About Ahmadinejad and Mousavi

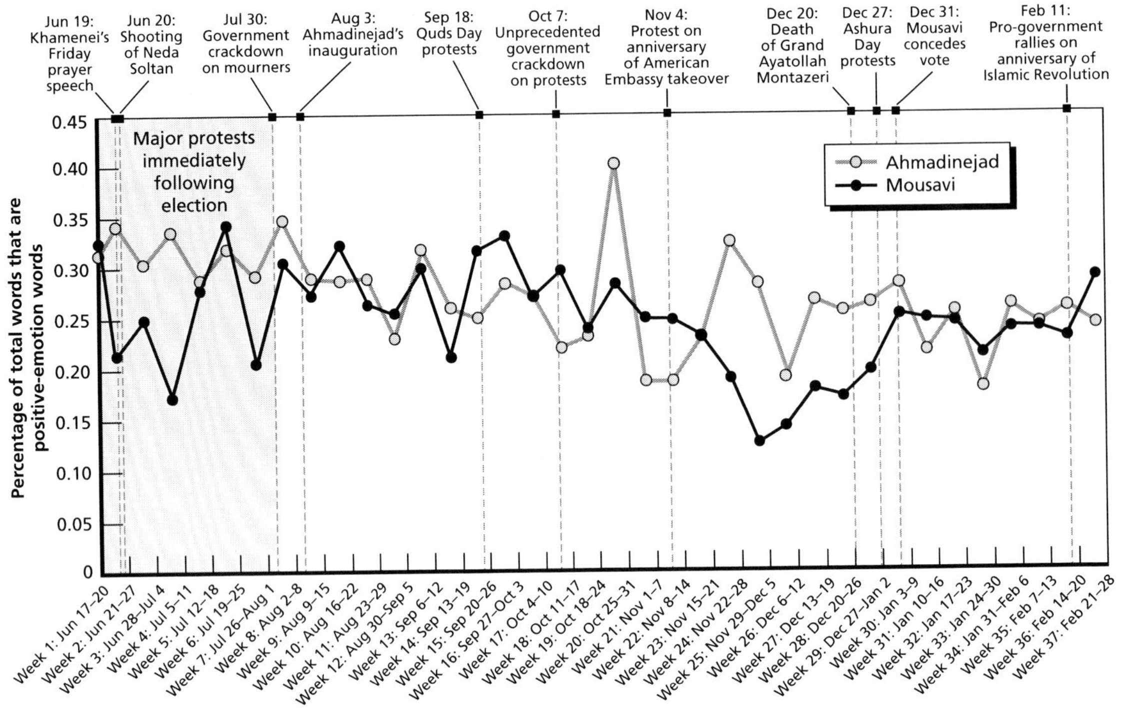

NOTES: The data points signify a ratio of positive-emotion words to total words across an entire week's worth of tweets. Significant events in the aftermath of the election are noted at the top of the figure.
RAND *TR1161-6.3*

object, concept, or person. Each usage may reflect a slight variation in a speaker's intentions, level of formality, or feelings about a given topic.

Several of these possibilities appear among the topics we explored in this study. For instance, typing "United States" is much more formal and precise than simply typing "US" or "U.S.A." This may suggest that people wrote the more formal usage when intending one meaning, and a more informal usage when meaning something else. It might also suggest differing language fluency, and perhaps, the characteristics of the speaker. Tweets referring to "United States" appeared to have a high degree of fluency, which may suggest that most people using this term were native speakers and therefore Westerners (probably Americans).

Other examples of topics and people that Twitter users commonly referred to in multiple ways included "Khameini" versus "Supreme Leader," "IRGC" versus "Revolutionary Guards," and "Israel" versus "Zionists." We analyzed public opinion in Iran related to these topics by (1) examining how people wrote (i.e., through a manual analysis of tweets) and (2) comparing LIWC indicators related to different phrasings that refer to the same topic (e.g., of "United States" or of "U.S."). Lack of data related to some phrasings precluded further analysis in this study. However, a future methodological exploration of phrasing differences might attempt to more directly compare these usages, looking for situational factors that affect when certain phrasings are used, and how public opinion varies when using different types of phrasing.

Figure 6.4
Seeming Patterns in Anxiety Expressed When Writing About Karroubi and Mousavi

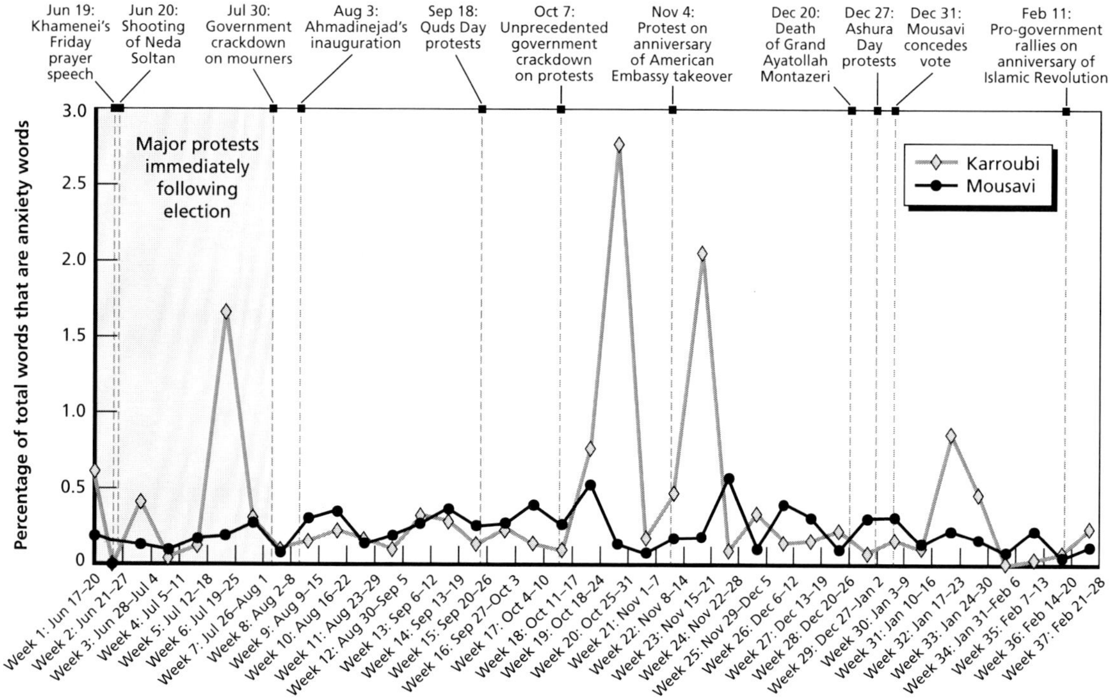

NOTES: The data points signify a ratio of anxiety words to total words across an entire week's worth of tweets. Significant events in the aftermath of the election are noted at the top of the figure.
RAND *TR1161-6.4*

Limitations of Automated Analysis Suggest That It Is a Complementary Approach to Manual Analysis

These examples illustrate the limits of using an automated approach to analyze texts. Given these limits, we recommend that policymakers regard linguistic indicators as signals of patterns in what people are writing that warrant further, manual scrutiny. Closer inspection may then reveal a meaningful change in the way people are discussing a particular topic, or they may also reveal a mundane factor that caused a spike in the data.

One way to reduce the odds of encountering mundane or spurious results consists of carefully constructing indicators with words that seem most useful in context and then testing those indicators for validity. For example, one might construct an "anxiety" indicator that either does or does not include the words "shame" and "ashamed," depending on the context in question. (In the case of LIWC analysis, one would do so by modifying LIWC's classification of anxiety words.) After constructing such an indicator, it would then be necessary to test it by using it to gather a pool of texts and then reading those texts to make sure that the indicator is capturing what it was designed to capture. Finally, it would be necessary to run spot-checks of the indicator over time to ensure that it continues to measure what it was designed to measure.

CHAPTER SEVEN

Next Steps: A Design for a Second Phase of This Program of Research

This report describes a novel method of analyzing politically oriented social media, but it represents only the first phase of a program of research. The results of this analysis regarding the 2009 Iranian presidential election offer initial insights into Iranian public opinion during this time period. With additional research, it will be possible to look ahead toward a future political event inside Iran, such as an upcoming presidential election, and to understand how public sentiment may shift regarding candidates and issues in the months leading up to that election. Additional research could also serve to validate more systematically the linguistic indicators used in the current project, and to prepare the methodology for use in other applications.

Looking Ahead Toward the 2013 Iranian Presidential Elections

Our use of the LIWC program in this phase of research was exploratory. Because LIWC has not been used in the Iranian context, nor widely used to study Twitter, our primary goal consisted of establishing that it generates reliable output. Having established several reliable indicators, we envision using LIWC as part of a multimethod study to answer timely policy questions. For example, the upcoming Iranian presidential election presents an opportunity to use LIWC to understand public sentiment toward the candidates and the issues of interest in the election. There is no straightforward way to study how people feel about candidates and political issues inside Iran because of the repressive political climate. For that reason, LIWC may serve as a valuable tool to gauge sentiment about "forbidden" political topics.

Our proposed research design for studying public opinion and mood surrounding the upcoming (June 2013) Iranian election includes several methodological techniques. In addition to including LIWC as a gauge of public sentiment, we could conduct manual analyses of the writings people post on social media. We could also conduct in-depth interviews of people traveling back-and-forth from Iran. Finally, we could content-analyze articles in Iranian news media regarding the candidates and topics of interest in the election. After obtaining data about public opinion and mood from each of these sources, we could compare and contrast the findings from each, which should provide as complete a picture as possible of how Iranian citizens feel about certain candidates and topics before the election.

Validating the Methodology

Having demonstrated a potential application of the current methodology, one possible next step consists of validating the methodology in a way that was not possible in the current project. To validate this methodology, we could compare the results of LIWC analysis against those of such existing forms of analysis, including elicitation of expert opinion, open-source analysis, and polling. As another example, the methodology entails drawing qualitative interpretations of LIWC output, which are quantitative in nature. Although such interpretations are grounded in the background literature on its development and validation, LIWC has not been validated for use with Twitter or with writings from Iran. To assist with our qualitative interpretation, we sampled tweets and reviewed them manually to determine whether Twitterers actually meant to communicate what our linguistic indicators suggested they were communicating. A more systematic follow-up project could conduct a thorough qualitative content analysis that entails reading all (or a representative sample of) tweets in a certain time period and categorizing them according to whether or not they substantiated interpretations suggested by the linguistic indicators. In addition, we could do more fine-grained analysis of what is meant when people use certain words. This could help to answer such questions as, for instance, whether people discussing an event use the word "we" to refer to nationalistic fervor or to personal relationships like "our family." Finally, a full qualitative analysis could examine what people mean when they use swear words and whether they swear to express something positive, to convey surprise, or to convey frustration and anger, as our initial qualitative analysis found in the current study.

Another way to validate the current methodology stems from the fact that it is based on research conducted in the West. This research has uncovered linkages between ways that people use language (e.g., pronouns) and their emotional states, as well as their desires to interact with others. The current project rests on an assumption that linkages demonstrated in Western contexts also apply to Iran. To validate this application, it would be ideal to replicate inside Iran the studies conducted in the West or, if that is not possible, among Iranians who travel back and forth between Iran and other countries. Examples of studies that could be replicated in this manner include those linking first-person singular pronouns with feelings of depression, or those linking first-person plural pronouns, second-person (singular and plural) pronouns, and third-person (singular and plural) pronouns with social processes. Finally, similar projects to be conducted in countries besides Iran would benefit from this type of background research in those countries as well.

A third way to validate our methodology consists of replicating the current study inside Iran over successive years to determine whether the methodology functions in the same way at different time periods. Because Iran will not hold another presidential election until June 2013, it could help to replicate the methodology before then. Such a replication could involve testing whether certain indicators reveal meaningful differences in how Iranians view different political leaders and topics, juxtaposing these differences with events on the ground.

Finally, we can validate the methodology by replicating the current study in other countries that have experienced political upheaval or traumatic experiences, such as Pakistan. Doing so would enable us to determine whether this methodology holds cross-cultural validity or whether it only applies to the Iranian context. In particular, a cross-cultural replication would enable us to examine whether linguistic patterns predict the outbreak of protests in countries other than Iran. If the current study can be replicated outside Iran, this replication would suggest that the methodology generalizes to multiple cultures, languages, and political situations.

Improving Current Aspects of the Methodology

We also envision improving specific aspects of the methodology in future work. First, while the scope of this work did not allow for statistical analysis, such techniques could be used to examine the power of linguistic features to forecast events over time, and to compare the effectiveness of features against one another. These could build on the foundation created by our initial, qualitative conclusions. Second, one problem we encountered in using our linguistic indicators stemmed from our efforts to examine sentiment about specific political figures. Sometimes, the indicators did not truly pinpoint sentiment about the individuals. One possible way to address this problem consists of using additional software (such as WordSmith, which finds patterns in text) in conjunction with LIWC to isolate pieces of text smaller than a tweet, such as a content word of interest (e.g., the name of a political figure) and the one or two words surrounding it. Doing so may make it possible to focus more narrowly on emotion words that refer strictly to the content word of interest. In addition, the field of sentiment analysis contains algorithms that may be more capable of measuring concordance of emotion words with a leader or topic than LIWC can. Bundling software with complementary functions in this manner parallels our recommended analytic approach of combining manual and computerized techniques.

A third way in which to improve the methodology consists of establishing base rates (i.e., average rates at which different types of words, such as positive-emotion words, swear words, etc., are used) for the Persian language or any other language of interest. Such base rates would enable us to determine objectively when people are using words at "high" levels or "low" levels. Base rates exist already for LIWC indicators—and for social media in particular (Pennebaker, Booth, and Francis, 2007)—but were developed in Western, English-speaking countries. Social psychologists have posited cultural differences in thought (Markus and Kitayama, 1991) that may be related to differences in language (Boroditsky, 2001). Because such differences may cause varying patterns of word usage, collecting a broader sample of texts from Iran or other countries, such as Pakistan or China, would enable us to develop culturally appropriate base rates.

Fourth, it may also be useful to differentiate between typical patterns of speech by topic (e.g., political vs. nonpolitical). For example, people may use different communication styles when chatting with a friend, as opposed to conducting a business meeting. Therefore, communication topics can be categorized, and usage base rates can be established for each of these categories.

Finally, we can improve the current methodology by improving our sampling process with regard to Twitter or other social media, such as blogs. In the current project, we chose to analyze tweets that carry the IranElection hashtag, because more people (inside and outside Iran) used that hashtag to tweet about the election than any other. However, one way to improve our methodology is to analyze tweets that carry different hashtags and either draw comparisons across the content of what people discuss or pool the tweets into one data set. Doing so would enable us to sample a broader cross-section of people using Twitter who are interested in different topics. Sampling social media to create an individual-level data set would also allow for finer-grained analyses and insight into whether public opinion was shifting among a static group or whether the changing composition of a population was responsible for changes in public opinion.

Concerning the future study of other social media, such as blogs, the ability to sample relevant texts poses an important methodological consideration. For example, potential approaches to blog sampling inherently compromise between generalizability and feasibility. A more systematic sampling approach would increase generalizability and, therefore, the validity of this method. One way to sample blogs more systematically might be to collaborate with hosting services to gather information about an entire population of blogs (e.g., all blogs focused on a specific topic). Doing so would allow a sample that represents every blog contained by the hosting services. Another possibility is to implement a snowball sampling process by creating an automated web crawler or "spider" that would start with an initial set of blogs and follow successive links from them to new sets of blogs; it would then generate a list of all blogs it encounters. Respondent-driven sampling (RDS), like snowball sampling, follows successive links to reveal additional members of the target population; however, RDS combines snowball techniques with statistical weighting models to produce samples that should be independent of biases in the initial sample (Heckathorn, 1997). This is a key consideration when sampling blogs, because initial sample bias may cause referral sampling methods to be ineffective, especially if the number of link iterations is insufficient. This is because blogs tend to link to similar blogs, leading to similar issues as with aggregator sites. Overcoming sampling issues such as these are crucial to any future social media analyses that wish to draw generalizable conclusions.

Expanding the Scope of the Current Work

To extend this current work, applying the methodology to other forms of social media is an obvious next step. For instance, we have conducted initial analyses of Iranian, Persian-language blogs, and of political leaders' Facebook postings, which are not reported here.

Other potential expansions of the current work may be topically oriented. A natural follow-up to this Iran-focused report would be to examine Iran-related topics of interest to policymakers that could not be covered in the current project, such as views of the Iranian economy or nuclear weapons. As in this study, it would be possible to track written expressions about these topics over time and to plot these trends against events on the ground. We could also extend the current research by looking across more than one country at a time to gauge the sentiments that social media users in each country express on topics of interest to them all. For example, using the current methodology, it is possible to compare sentiments expressed across Iran, Pakistan, and other countries on topics including the United States, nuclear weapons, and domestic political issues. Other extensions of the current research could focus on Asian countries that are high on the national security agenda, such as China and Taiwan, or on Middle Eastern countries where political protests in early 2011 were reportedly influenced by social media use, such as Egypt and Tunisia. However, censorship of the Internet or of social media in these countries may present additional methodological barriers.

In addition to policy-oriented extensions of the current work, other extensions can focus on methodological aspects. For example, one such extension consists of building our own indicators of words that may be meaningful in predicting protests or other types of events. Specifically, we can incorporate words such as "protest" or "demonstration" in such a dictionary to examine how effectively these words predict protests. Developing clusters of indicators, based on individual indicators that behaved similarly, could also be beneficial.

Another idea stems from the fact that many tweets contained links to YouTube videos. Consequently, our program of research into social media can explore not only those media that are primarily text-based (e.g., Twitter), but also the content associated with these video sites (e.g., YouTube). A first step in analyzing video-based social media would be to identify the number of users who reference a YouTube video and possibly the actual video itself (if the URL is embedded in the text). Other analyses focused on YouTube could examine transcripts of the videos, comments made in response to the videos, or the referring sources from which they were linked. The text collected from any of these sources would be content analyzed using LIWC.

A final way to extend the current methodology is to build a real-time tracking tool for social media texts. Such a tool could automatically download texts as they are posted, run them through a parsing algorithm, and place them into a database for processing through LIWC (or other software). Using such a tool, it would be possible to view and analyze patterns in written texts almost as quickly as they unfold. Given the policy relevance of our findings, these recommendations for validation and extensions of the methodology illustrate the potential of analyzing social media to understand public mood and opinion in various populations of interest.

APPENDIX

Additional Details Regarding Methodology: Data Collection and Analysis

Data Collection Tasks: Collecting and Storing Social Media Texts

Twitter Archive

We simply downloaded the entire IranElection archive from TwapperKeeper.com as a single compressed file.[1] Uncompressing this file yielded a single text file with all the tweets, including text and metadata.

Database to Store Twitter Texts

We built a database to store the Twitter texts, along with their associated metadata. These data were loaded into the database using shell and Perl scripts operating on the output of data parsers (e.g., tweet date, user, text extracted from the tweets) that we also built. The database contained several tables that stored subsets of data, each of which contained common variables (e.g., tweet date, Twitter user ID), so that they could be linked together to explore different subgroups of the sample. We then built a web interface to query the database. This allowed us to have easy access to any subset of data, simply by selecting any of several parameters. For instance, we could choose a subset of tweets from August 2009 containing the keywords "Supreme Leader," or all tweets from July 1, 2009.

Data Analysis Tasks: Generating Quantitative Indicators and Qualitative Interpretations

Preparing and Cleaning the Social Media Texts

Translation of Twitter Text. The Twitter data from the IranElection archive was almost entirely in English and did not need to be translated.

Cleaning the Texts. Text intended for input into the LIWC software must be appropriately formatted and cleaned of nonstandard variations, which will be described in more detail below. Given that online sources constitute the primary supply of social media text, much of the necessary data cleaning involved removing extraneous HTML tags.[2]

LIWC analysis is not affected by many common text variations, such as punctuation, abbreviations, and misspellings. Because LIWC simply counts individual words, grammar

---

[1] As of late 2011, the IranElection archive is no longer available for download from TwapperKeeper.com.

[2] We retained and converted HTML tags that indicate special characters in the text. For example, """ was changed to a quotation mark, and " " was changed to a hyphen.

and sentence structure do not affect the analysis. LIWC also converts all text files to lower case before processing them, so that capitalization does not affect the analysis. Occasional misspellings are not a significant issue, especially with thousands of texts tweets in which the majority of words will be spelled correctly. Validation research on an earlier version of LIWC, along with a German-language version, showed that spelling errors do not significantly affect the word category ratios (Cindy K. Chung, personal communication, 2010).

To ensure the maximum possible accuracy, however, we decided to clean the data. Our parsing program made the following changes to the Twitter text:[3]

- *Spelling.* Spelling errors were corrected to conform to standard American English (although the default LIWC dictionary also contains most British English spellings).
- *Abbreviations.* Meaningful abbreviations were spelled out (e.g., "Jan" was changed to "January," "w/" to "with"). Less common abbreviations or acronyms, such as "AT&T," were left unchanged.
- *End-of-sentence markers.* Periods that did not denote ends of sentences were removed. This was because LIWC counts some common abbreviations (e.g., "Dr.," "Ms.," "U.S.A.") as multiple sentences unless the periods are removed. If this had not been done, counts for the words-per-sentence (WPS) category—which is based on the number of times that LIWC detects end-of-sentence markers[4]—may have been inaccurate. For example, "U.S.," referring to the United States, became "US" when the periods were removed. (And because this particular abbreviation could be mistaken for the first-person plural pronoun "us," it was changed to "USA.")
- *Contractions.* Common verb contractions (e.g., "don't," "won't," "isn't," "I'm," "we'd," "you're") exist in the LIWC dictionary and did not need to be changed.
- *Time markers.* Because "a.m." without the periods is a verb ("am"), time markers were changed, from "6 am" and "7:30 p.m.," for example, to "6am" and "7:30pm," respectively.
- *Hyphens.* LIWC reads words that begin or end with hyphens as part of the word itself. For example the LIWC dictionary lists "self-esteem" as a meaningful word. But this means that LIWC will list hyphenated phrases such as "this-or-that" as a single word. To correct this, phrases such as "this-or-that" were changed to "this - or - that." Blanks were also inserted on either side of hyphens intended as dashes between words—such as "we went to the store-I don't know why"—because LIWC would erroneously count "store-I" as one word.
- *Emoticons.* Text emoticons are used to indicate the tone of online communications. To ensure that LIWC captured these expressed emotions, we converted these combinations of letters and punctuation to actual words that would be categorized into LIWC's emotion categories. For example, ":-)" and ";-)" were converted to "happy," and ":(" and "=(" were converted to "sad."

Using the LIWC Software to Generate the Core Quantitative Analysis

After preparing and cleaning the texts in our Twitter sample and selecting the LIWC word categories to analyze, we processed the texts with the LIWC content analysis software. When

---

[3] We based these changes on data cleaning recommendations in the LIWC 2007 Operator's Manual (Pennebaker, Booth, and Francis, 2007).

[4] End-of-sentence markers include all periods, question marks, and exclamation points.

provided text inputs, LIWC generates an output file that contains a set of ratios for each specific word category covered by the program. This set of ratios constitutes the core quantitative data used to analyze the social media texts. Each ratio within a set is determined by comparing the count of words in a particular category against the total number of words in a text or set of texts. Take, for example, the category of positive-emotion words: LIWC has an internal dictionary, and there are 406 words in that dictionary that are included in the category "positive-emotion words." When fed a piece of text, LIWC first counts the number of total words in the entire text. Then, it counts how many of those words (e.g., "happy," "good") fall into the category of "positive-emotion words." Finally, LIWC calculates a ratio of the percentage of the total words in that piece of text that are positive-emotion words. It outputs these ratios for each of 76 different word categories. Of note is the fact that the same word may be counted in multiple categories. For example, the word "it" would be coded specifically as an "impersonal pronoun" but also as a "pronoun" and a "linguistic function word." The counts of all those LIWC categories would be incremented accordingly.

The raw texts in our samples were very granular, existing as individual tweets. To manage this, we took advantage of LIWC's ability to run batches of data and produce either a single output (i.e., set of ratios) for the total batch or individual outputs for each text, or even section of text. Whichever output a researcher chooses depends on the unit of analysis that is most appropriate for the data set—in this case, week or day. We therefore aggregated the tweets by time period. Broad trends over the entire nine-month period following the elections required aggregation by week. In other words, we combined Twitter texts for each one-week period to produce a single set of LIWC ratios for that week. To examine shorter timeframes (i.e., leading up to given political events and in response to them), it may be more appropriate to aggregate by day. These time-based units of analysis were particularly apposite for studying Twitter—first, because individual tweets contained too little text,[5] and second, because there were too many individual users (972–43,567, depending on the week) to allow meaningful analyses by individual user.

As another part of this step in our methodology, we linked the LIWC output to political topics. To do this, we filtered the aggregated data by selected keywords so that we could see patterns in word usage around a specific topic and thus draw conclusions about public opinion and mood associated with that topic.[6] For example, our entire Twitter dataset consisted of tweets that had self-identified as being about the Iranian presidential election. Of these, some tweets mentioned, for example, "Obama." Because each of those tweets contained so little text, we assumed a relationship between the LIWC result (e.g., use of positive- or negative-emotion words) for the subset of tweets that mentioned "Obama" and the subject of President Obama—that is, we inferred that the subset of tweets was "about" Obama, even though it is likely that some tweets that mentioned Obama, and thus were in the subset, were not about

[5] At minimum, a word count of 100 words per text file should be considered. Text files with fewer words than that should be excluded or aggregated (Cindy K. Chung, personal communication, July, 2010).

[6] Some keywords—"Ahmadinejad," for example—are often abbreviated or misspelled. In certain cases, we used a keyword stem (e.g., "Ahmadi") to capture additional variations, and thus more usages, of those keywords. We also inspected the tweets themselves to verify that the stems captured the appropriate tweets.

Obama.[7] We stored the aggregated data of LIWC outputs in the database, along with other metadata.

Conducting the Qualitative Analysis of the LIWC Output

After obtaining all of our quantitative output from LIWC, we analyzed these data qualitatively. This entailed plotting the trends in our quantitative output against a timeline of events on the ground inside Iran so that we could determine whether they coincided with (or even forecasted) these events. We first plotted overall trends in the use of certain words that signify mood to examine how public mood changed over the nine months after the election. Then, we isolated tweets containing certain keywords of interest (such as "Khamenei" or "Mousavi") and at least one word contained in one of our LIWC indicators (such as the "sadness" indicator, "positive emotion" indicator, etc.). Based on these samples of text, we plotted trends in the sentiment expressed surrounding each keyword to examine how public sentiment on each topic changed over time.

To be meaningful, LIWC outputs—proportions of usage for a particular word category—require a point of comparison. First, usage may be compared *within* each word category, either (1) across time periods (i.e., tracking trends) or (2) against known baselines for that category. Within-category comparisons allow for interpretation and conclusions about that particular category for a given population.

Second, usage may be compared *across* word categories to better understand the relationships between them. The usage patterns, however, should not be directly compared across categories. In other words, it is not possible to simply compare relative usage proportions between two categories and conclude that a given population is, for example, happier than it is sad. This is because people naturally use words in differing proportions. Thus for any given word category, it is the *changes* in usage patterns that we compared against other categories, rather than directly comparing proportions themselves.

We looked at a range of patterns and interpreted them in the following ways:

Overall trends. Changes in word use over extended periods of time may suggest a general shift toward some new state, and perhaps even that these trends are solidifying into a more stable state—that is, moving toward a "new normal." For instance, a subset of individuals in a population may be coalescing, their increased usage of second-person plural words suggesting the formation of a collective identity.

Patterns around events. Word-usage changes that occur around significant events may offer insight into public opinion about that event. For example, these patterns may be a dip just before an event or a gradual falling-off after the event. Different patterns may be observed for anticipated events (e.g., holidays) than for unanticipated events (e.g., outbreak of war). Note that although events coinciding with patterns in writing may reflect public opinion about those events, these correlations cannot be used to determine causal relationships.

Spikes and dips. Sudden changes in word usage may indicate short-term responses or reactions to a specific event or action. These dramatic changes in word usage may indicate a sharp increase (or decrease) in interest about a particular topic, or a significant psychological response to a given event.

---

[7] We briefly discuss in Chapter Seven techniques that may be more sensitive methods of determining whether public opinion is indeed linked to a given topic.

Gradual increases or declines over a shorter period. Gradual changes in word usage that occur over relatively short periods of time may be related to factors other than a particular event, although the shortened time period makes it unclear whether a more permanent or long-term change is occurring. It may be useful to consider what may have happened during a certain time that could have caused, for example, feelings of insecurity to level off.

Comparisons between trends. When comparing trends, some word categories will naturally track each other. For instance, usage of first-person singular, which suggests depressive and other negative states, may closely follow usage of negative emotion word categories, such as "sad." In addition, there may be naturally inverse interactions between trends, such as between positive and negative emotion categories.

Less obvious or counterintuitive patterns should not be overlooked. For instance, it may seem that plural pronouns (indicating, for example, heightened social contact) naturally correlate with positive emotions, given that social interaction is generally thought to be comforting. Yet in certain political contexts—such as in angry protests or demonstrations—a sense of collective may correlate with anger and other strong emotions.

Comparisons against baselines. Two types of baseline values may be employed to determine changes in LIWC outputs. First, base rates of general usage have been established for each of the LIWC word categories. These base rates differentiate between specific types of writings, such as emotional writings, science articles, blogs, novels, and talking, but not tweets (Pennebaker et al., 2007b). Thus, LIWC outputs may be compared against base rates from the most appropriate source for the given text.

Note, however, that these base rates were developed from English-speaking, primarily Western countries (the United States, the United Kingdom, Canada, and New Zealand). This is important because, such as in the present research on Iran, the base rates may not accurately reflect the possibility that word usage patterns vary across cultures or languages. Culturally appropriate base rates remain an area for future research, as does cross-cultural language use in general.

Given that culturally appropriate base rates do not yet exist, in this study we did not compare tweets against base rates of usage. Rather, we focused on the other type of baseline value: changes in LIWC outputs over time. Word usage from a time period of interest may be compared against usage from another time period. As with events, attributes from the two time periods may be compared to determine what may have contributed to changing word usage. We also compared LIWC outputs concerning one topic (e.g., "Obama") with those concerning related topics (e.g., "Ahmadinejad") to gain further perspective on each topic.

References

"22 Bahman Protests: Iranian Opposition Planning Demonstrations on Anniversary of Revolution," *Huffpost World*, February 10, 2010. As of November 3, 2011:
http://www.huffingtonpost.com/2010/02/10/22-bahman-protests-irania_n_457851.html

Alpers, Georg W., Andrew J. Winzelberg, Catherine Classen, Heidi Roberts, Parvati Dev, Cheryl Koopman, and C. Barr Taylor, "Evaluation of Computerized Text Analysis in an Internet Breast Cancer Support Group," *Computers in Human Behavior*, Vol. 21, 2005, pp. 361–376.

Alvarez, Steve, "CENTCOM Team Engages 'Bloggers,'" U.S. Department of Defense, American Foreign Press Service, March 2, 2006. As of November 3, 2011:
http://www.defense.gov/news/newsarticle.aspx?id=15287

Amos, Deborah, "1 Year Later, Iran's Opposition Still Relies on Internet," *NPR*, June 9, 2010. As of November 3, 2011:
http://www.npr.org/templates/story/story.php?storyId=127586505

Applebaum, A., "Prepare for War with Iran—in Case Israel Strikes," *Washington Post*, February 23, 2010. As of November 3, 2011:
http://www.washingtonpost.com/wp-dyn/content/article/2010/02/22/AR2010022203528.html

Athanasiadis, Iason, "Accused of Spying: Journalist Iason Athanasiadis Tells of His Time in Iranian Jail," *World News*, July 12, 2009. As of November 3, 2011:
http://www.telegraph.co.uk/news/worldnews/middleeast/iran/5805673/
Accused-of-spying-journalist-Iason-Athanasiadis-tells-of-his-time-in-Iranian-jail.html

Ayoub, M., "Arba'in," *Encyclopedia Iranica*, online edition, 1986. As of November 3, 2011:
http://www.iranica.com/articles/arbain-fortieth-day-after-asura-q

Back, Mitja, Albrecht Kufner, and Boris Egloff, "The Emotional Timeline of September 11, 2001," *Psychological Science*, Vol. 21, No. 10, 2010, pp. 1417–1419.

———, "Automatic or the People? Anger on September 11, 2001, and Lessons Learned for the Analysis of Large Digital Data Sets," *Psychological Science*, Vol. 20, No. 10, 2011, pp. 1–2.

"Basij Militia," *New York Times*, June 19, 2009. As of November 3, 2011:
http://topics.nytimes.com/topics/reference/timestopics/organizations/b/basij_militia/index.html

BBC News, "Iran Leader's Comments Attacked," October 27, 2005. As of November 3, 2011:
http://news.bbc.co.uk/2/hi/4378948.stm

———, "Blogosphere Sees Healthy Growth," November 8, 2006. As of November 3, 2011:
http://news.bbc.co.uk/2/hi/6129496.stm

———, "Shots Fired at Huge Iran Protest," June 15, 2009a. As of November 3, 2011:
http://news.bbc.co.uk/2/hi/middle_east/8101098.stm

———, "Obama Refuses to "Meddle" in Iran," June 19, 2009b. As of November 3, 2011:
http://news.bbc.co.uk/2/hi/8104362.stm

———, "Obama Says Honduras Coup Illegal," June 29, 2009c. As of November 3, 2011:
http://news.bbc.co.uk/2/hi/americas/8125292.stm

———, "Iran Lifts Block on SMS Texting," July 2, 2009d. As of November 3, 2011:
http://news.bbc.co.uk/2/hi/middle_east/8131095.stm

———, "Iran Police Clash with Protesters," November 4, 2009e. As of November 3, 2011:
http://news.bbc.co.uk/2/hi/middle_east/8341631.stm

———, "Iran Witness: I Saw People Shot," December 27, 2009f. As of November 3, 2011:
http://news.bbc.co.uk/2/hi/middle_east/8432066.stm

———, "Mousavi Statement: Excerpts," January 1, 2010a. As of November 3, 2011:
http://news.bbc.co.uk/2/hi/middle_east/8437322.stm

———, "Hundreds of Thousands Back Iran Revolution," February 11, 2010b. As of November 3, 2011:
http://news.bbc.co.uk/2/hi/middle_east/8509765.stm

———, "Iranian Leader Accuses US of Plotting Against Iran," March 21, 2010c. As of November 3, 2011:
http://news.bbc.co.uk/2/hi/americas/8578976.stm

———, "Iran Country Profile," May 11, 2011. As of November 3, 2011:
http://news.bbc.co.uk/2/hi/middle_east/country_profiles/790877.stm#facts

Betteridge, A. H., P. G. Kreyenbroek, and K. Hitchins, "Festivals iii, iv, v," *Encyclopedia Iranica*, online edition, 1999. As of November 3, 2011:
http://www.iranica.com/articles/festivals-iii-iv-v

Boroditsky, L., "Does Language Shape Thought? Mandarin and English Speakers' Conception of Time," *Cognitive Psychology*, Vol. 43, No. 1, 2001, pp. 1–22.

Bureau of International Information Programs, U.S. Department of State, *Digital Outreach Team*, 2009. As of November 3, 2011:
http://www.state.gov/documents/organization/116709.pdf

Butters, Andrew Lee, "Iran's Karroubi Tries a More Confrontational Approach," *Time Magazine*, August 24, 2009.

Cashmore, Pete, "Iran Blocks Facebook to Silence Presidential Rival," *Mashable*, May 23, 2009. As of November 3, 2011:
http://mashable.com/2009/05/23/iran-blocks-facebook/

Cellan-Jones, Rory, "Hi-Tech Helps Iranian Monitoring," *Wall Street Journal*, Middle East News, June 22, 2009. As of November 3, 2011:
http://news.bbc.co.uk/2/hi/technology/8112550.stm

Central Intelligence Agency, "Iran," *The World Factbook*, Washington, D.C.: CIA, 2010.

Chung, Cindy K., Clinton Jones, Alexander Liu, and James W. Pennebaker, *Predicting Success and Failure in Weight Loss Blogs Through Natural Language Use*, Austin, Tex.: University of Texas, 2008.

Chung, Cindy K., and James W. Pennebaker, "The Psychological Function of Function Words," in Klaus Fiedler, ed., *Social Communication: Frontiers of Social Psychology*, New York: Psychology Press, 2007, pp. 343–359.

Cohn, Michael A., Matthias R. Mehl, and James W. Pennebaker, "Linguistic Markers of Psychological Change Surrounding September 11, 2001," *Psychological Science*, Vol. 15, 2004, pp. 687–693.

Cooper, Helene, and David Sanger, "Obama Condemns Iran's Iron Fist Against Protests," *New York Times*, June 23, 2009. As of November 3, 2011:
http://www.nytimes.com/2009/06/24/us/politics/24webobama.html

Cyberwar4iran, "Help Protect Iranian Protesters by Tracking Down and Disabling the Regime Crowdsourcing Websites," June 28, 2009. As of November 3, 2011:
http://cyberwar4iran.blogspot.com/2009/06/how-to-help-take-down-gerdabir-in-5.html

Elson, Sara Beth, and Alireza Nader, *What Do Iranians Think? A Survey of Attitudes on the United States, the Nuclear Program, and the Economy*, Santa Monica, Calif.: RAND Corporation, TR-910-OSD, 2011. As of November 3, 2011:
http://www.rand.org/pubs/technical_reports/TR910.html

Erdbrink, Thomas, "Iran's Mousavi Issues Charter, Seeks Radical Reforms on Clerical Rule," *Washington Post*, June 16, 2010. As of November 3, 2011:
http://www.washingtonpost.com/wp-dyn/content/article/2010/06/16/AR2010061603497.html

Esfandiari, Golnaz, "Tehran Sees Protests Despite Officials' Warnings," *Radio Free Europe, Radio Liberty*, July 9, 2009. As of November 3, 2011:
http://www.rferl.org/content/Hundreds_Protest_In_Tehran_Despite_Officials_Warnings/1773423.html

Fassihi, Farnaz, "Iranian Crackdown Goes Global," *Wall Street Journal*, Middle East News, December 3, 2009. As of November 3, 2011:
http://online.wsj.com/article/NA_WSJ_PUB:SB125978649644673331.html

Fathi, Nazila, "Student Protests After Quds Day," *New York Times*, July 9, 2009a.

———, "Iranian Court Shuts Down 3 Pro-Reform Newspapers as Dissent Continues to Simmer," *New York Times*, October 7, 2009b.

———, "Clashes with Police Reported in Iran," *New York Times*, December 23, 2009c.

Foreign Affairs Committee of the National Council of Resistance of Iran, "Activities of the IRGC to Tackle 'Soft' Threats," *Foreign Affairs Committee of the National Council of Resistance of Iran*, May 20, 2010. As of November 3, 2011:
http://ncr-iran.org/en/news/terrorism-a-fundamentalism/8172-activities-of-the-irgc-to-tackle-soft-threatsWir

Fredrickson, Barbara, "The Value of Positive Emotions," *American Scientist*, Vol. 91, 2003, pp. 330–335.

Freedom House, *Freedom on the Net: A Global Assessment of Internet and Digital Media*, Washington, D.C., 2009.

———, *Freedom on the Net 2011: Iran*, Washington, D.C., 2011. As of November 16, 2011:
http://www.freedomhouse.org/images/File/FotN/Iran2011.pdf

Friedman, T., "Power to the (Blogging) People," *New York Times*, September 14, 2010. As of November 3, 2011:
http://www.nytimes.com/2010/09/15/opinion/
15friedman.html?_r=1&scp=2&sq=China%20blogosphere&st=Search

Gerdab, "Taking Down Gerdab.ir," June 27, 2009. As of November 3, 2011:
http://sites.google.com/site/gerdabdeath/index

Gile, Krista, and Mark S. Handcock, *Respondent-Driven Sampling: An Assessment of Current Methodology*, unpublished manuscript, 2010.

Gortner, Eva-Maria, and James W. Pennebaker, "The Archival Anatomy of a Disaster: Media Coverage and Community-Wide Health Effects of the Texas A&M Bonfire Tragedy," *Journal of Social and Clinical Psychology*, Vol. 22, 2003, pp. 580–603.

Great Iran, "A Few Words to the Gerdab Ppl," Nedasites, June 26, 2009. As of November 3, 2011:
http://sites.google.com/site/nedasites/news/afewwordstogerdabppl

Haaretz Service and the Associated Press, "Ahmadinejad: Opposition Rally a Zionist, U.S. Masquerade," *Haaretz.com*, December 29, 2009. As of November 3, 2011:
http://www.haaretz.com/news/ahmadinejad-opposition-rally-a-zionist-u-s-masquerade-1.1156

Hancock, Jeffrey T., David I. Beaver, Cindy K. Chung, Joey Frazee, James W. Pennebaker, Art Graesser, and Zhiqiang Cai, "Social Language Processing: A Framework for Analyzing the Communication of Terrorists and Authoritarian Regimes," *Behavioral Sciences of Terrorism and Political Aggression*, Vol. 2, No. 2, May 2010, pp. 108–132.

Hancock, Jeffrey T., Lauren E. Curry, Saurabh Goorha, and Michael Woodworth, "On Lying and Being Lied to: A Linguistic Analysis of Deception in Computer-Mediated Communication," *Discourse Processes*, Vol. 45, No. 1, 2008, pp. 1–23.

Heckathorn, Douglas, "Respondent-Driven Sampling: A New Approach to the Study of Hidden Populations," *Social Problems*, Vol. 44, No. 2, 1997, pp. 174–199.

———, "Respondent-Driven Sampling II: Deriving Valid Population Estimates from Chain-Referral Samples of Hidden Populations," *Social Problems*, Vol. 49, No. 1, 2002, pp. 11–34.

Helft, Miguel, "Amid Iran Turmoil, Google Adds Persian to Translation Service," *New York Times*, July 19, 2009. As of November 3, 2011:
http://bits.blogs.nytimes.com/2009/06/19/amid-iran-turmoil-google-adds-persian-to-translation-service/

Iran, Asr, and Peykeiran, "Javad Larijani Uses Racial Slur in Reference to Obama," *Frontline*, tehranbureau, June 24, 2010. As of November 3, 2011:
http://www.pbs.org/wgbh/pages/frontline/tehranbureau/2010/01/weekend-headlines-1.html

"Iran: Opposition and Hard-Liners Get Ready for 22 Bahman Confrontations," February 7, 2010. As of November 3, 2011:
http://latimesblogs.latimes.com/babylonbeyond/2010/02/iran-22-bahman-revolution-election-ahmadinejad-mousavi-khatami-khamenei-karroubi.html

Iranian Lawyers for the Green Movement, blog, no date. As of November 15, 2011:
http://greenlawyers.wordpress.com/

"Iranian Protest Is Grassroots and Unstoppable, Say Activists," *The Times, The Sunday Times*, December 30, 2009.

"Islamic Revolutionary Guards Corps," *New York Times*, October 9, 2009. As of November 3, 2011:
http://topics.nytimes.com/top/reference/timestopics/organizations/i/islamic_revolutionary_guard_corps/index.html?scp=1&sq=Iranian%20Revolutionary%20Guards%20Corps&st=cse

Jardin, Xeni, "Iran SMS Networks "Mysteriously" Fail Right Before Elections," *BoingBoing*, June 13, 2009. As of November 3, 2011:
http://www.boingboing.net/2009/06/13/iran-sms-networks-my.html

Kahn, Jeffrey, Renee Tobin, Audra Massey, and Jennifer Anderson, "Measuring Emotional Expression with the Linguistic Inquiry and Word Count," *American Journal of Psychology*, Vol. 120, No. 2, 2007, pp. 263–286.

Karroubi, Mehdi, "Mehdi Karroubi's Profile," Facebook, June 22, 2009. As of November 3, 2011:
http://www.facebook.com/pages/Mehdi-Karroubi/68765459902?v=feed&story_fbid=96406985955&ref=mf

Keila, P. S., and D. B. Skillicorn, "Detecting Unusual Email Communication," unpublished manuscript, Kingston, Ontario, Canada: Queen's University, 2005.

Kelly, J., and B. Etling, *Mapping Iran's Online Public: Political and Culture in the Persian Blogosphere*, Cambridge, Mass.: Harvard University, Berkman Center for Internet and Society, 2008.

Kornacki, Steve, ed., "The Revolution Will Be Blogged," *Salon*, March 6, 2006. As of November 3, 2011:
http://www.salon.com/news/feature/2006/03/06/iranian_bloggers/

Kwan, Eric, "Launching Facebook in Persian," Facebook Blog, June 18, 2009. As of November 3, 2011:
http://blog.facebook.com/blog.php?post=97122772130

Landler, Mark, "Obama Resists Calls for a Tougher Stance on Iran," *New York Times*, June 19, 2009. As of November 3, 2011:
http://www.nytimes.com/2009/06/20/world/middleeast/20policy.html

Macer, Tim, and Sheila Wilson, "Dipping a Toe in Social Media Analysis," *Quirk's Marketing Research Review*, Vol. 25, No. 5, 2011, pp. 60–74.

Markus, H. R., and S. Kitayama, "Culture and the Self: Implications for Cognition, Emotion, and Motivation," *Psychological Review*, Vol. 98, No. 2, 1991, pp. 224–253.

Masnick, Mike, "Iran Sends Warning SMS Messages to Potential Protestors," Wireless by techdirt, June 16, 2010. As of November 3, 2011:
http://www.techdirt.com/blog/wireless/articles/20100614/1905389816.shtml

Milani, Abbas, "Iran Primer: The Green Movement," *Tehran Bureau*, October 27, 2010. As of November 3, 2011:
http://www.pbs.org/wgbh/pages/frontline/tehranbureau/2010/10/iran-primer-the-green-movement.html

NBC News, "Iran Marks Revolution with Protest Crackdown," February 11, 2010. As of November 3, 2011:
http://www.msnbc.msn.com/id/35345722/ns/world_news-mideast/n_africa/

Newman, Matthew L., Carla J. Groom, Lori D. Handelman, and James W. Pennebaker, "Gender Differences in Language Use: An Analysis of 14,000 Text Samples," *Discourse Processes*, Vol. 45, 2008, pp. 211–236.

Newman, Matthew L., James W. Pennebaker, Diane S. Berry, and Jane M. Richards, "Lying Words: Predicting Deception from Linguistic Styles," *Personality and Social Psychology Bulletin*, Vol. 29, No. 5, 2003, pp. 665–675.

Nikou, Semira N., "Timeline of Iran's Political Events," *The Iran Primer, United States Institute of Peace*, 2010. As of November 3, 2011:
http://iranprimer.usip.org/resource/timeline-irans-political-events

Niteowl, "Transcript of Ayatollah Khamenei's Friday Speech," *PasteBay*, June 19, 2009. As of November 3, 2011:
http://pastebay.com/23186

"Obama, Honduras, and Iran," *The Economist*, Ideas Arena, June 30, 2009. As of November 3, 2011:
http://www.economist.com/blogs/democracyinamerica/2009/06/obama_honduras_and_iran

Parr, Ben, "Mindblowing #Iranelection Stats: 221,744 Tweets per Hour at Peak," *Mashable*, June 17, 2009a. As of November 3, 2011:
http://mashable.com/2009/06/17/iranelection-crisis-numbers/

———, "Facebook Releases Persian Translation for #Iranelection Crisis," *Mashable*, June 18, 2009b. As of November 3, 2011:
http://mashable.com/2009/06/18/facebook-persian/

Pennebaker, James W., Roger J. Booth, and Martha E. Francis, *Linguistic Inquiry and Word Count: LIWC2007—Operator's Manual*, Austin, Tex.: LIWC.net, 2007.

Pennebaker, James W., and Cindy K. Chung, "Tracking the Social Dynamics of Responses to Terrorism: Language, Behavior, and the Internet," in S. Wessely and V. N. Krasnov, eds., *Psychological Responses to the New Terrorism: A NATO Russia Dialogue*, Amsterdam, The Netherlands: IOS Press, 2005, pp. 159–170.

———, "Computerized Text Analysis of al-Qaeda Statements," in Klaus Krippendorff and Mary Angela Bock, eds., *A Content Analysis Reader*, Thousand Oaks, Calif.: Sage, 2008, pp. 453–466.

Pennebaker, James W., Cindy K. Chung, M. Ireland, A. Gonzales, and Roger J. Booth, *The Development and Psychometric Properties of LIWC2007*, Austin, Tex.: LIWC.net, 2007.

Pennebaker, James W., Tracy J. Mayne, and Martha E. Francis, "Linguistic Predictors of Adaptive Bereavement," *Journal of Personality and Social Psychology*, Vol. 72, No. 4, 1997, pp. 863–871.

Pennebaker, James W., Matthias R. Mehl, and Kate G. Niederhoffer, "Psychological Aspects of Natural Language Use: Our Words, Our Selves," *Annual Review of Psychology*, Vol. 54, 2003, pp. 547–577.

Pennebaker, James W., Richard B. Slatcher, and Cindy K. Chung, "Linguistic Markers of Psychological State Through Media Interviews: John Kerry and John Edwards in 2004, Al Gore in 2000," *Analyses of Social Issues and Public Policy*, Vol. 5, No. 1, 2005, pp. 197–204.

Peskin, Doron, "Iranian Election Campaign Costs Millions," *Israel Business*, June 13, 2009. As of November 3, 2011:
http://www.ynetnews.com/articles/0,7340,L-3730357,00.html

Pollack, Kenneth M., *The Persian Puzzle: The Conflict Between Iran and America*, New York: Random House, 2004.

PressTV, "Larijani: Obama Is International Villain," September 25, 2010. As of November 3, 2011:
http://www.presstv.ir/detail/143973.html

RAND National Security Research Division, "Using Twitter to Track Public Sentiment in Iran After the Contested 2009 Election," 2011. As of November 4, 2011:
http://www.rand.org/nsrd/ndri/tracking-iranian-public-sentiment.html

Reporters Without Borders, *Internet Enemies*, Paris, France, March 12, 2009.

Rhoads, Christopher, and Loretta Chao, "Iran's Web Spying Aided by Western Technology," *Wall Street Journal*, June 23, 2009. As of November 3, 2011:
http://online.wsj.com/article/SB124562668777335653.html

Rhoads, Christopher, Chip Cummins, and Jessica Vascellaro, "Iran to Suspend Google's Email," *Wall Street Journal*, Middle East News, February 10, 2010. As of November 3, 2011:
http://online.wsj.com/article/NA_WSJ_PUB:SB10001424052748704140104575057621649270154.html

Rude, Stephanie, Eva-Maria Gortner, and J. W. Pennebaker, "Language Use of Depressed and Depression-Vulnerable College Students," *Cognition and Emotion*, Vol. 18, No. 8, 2004, pp. 1121–1133.

Sadjadpour, Karim, *Reading Khamenei: The World View of Iran's Most Powerful Leader*, Washington, D.C.: Carnegie Endowment for International Peace, 2008.

Sahimi, Muhammad, "Grand Ayatollah Montazeri's Fatwa: An Unfair Supreme Leader Is Illegitimate," *Frontline*, Tehran Bureau, July 12, 2009. As of November 3, 2011:
http://www.pbs.org/wgbh/pages/frontline/tehranbureau/2009/07/grand-ayatollah-montazeris-fatwa.html

Segan, Sascha, "Learning from Iran's Twitter Revolution," *PCMag*, June 18, 2009. As of November 3, 2011:
http://www.pcmag.com/article2/0,2817,2348924,00.asp

Simmons, Rachel, Dianne Chambless, and Peter C. Gordon, "How Do Hostile and Emotionally Overinvolved Relatives View Relationships? What Relatives' Pronoun Use Tells Us," *Family Process*, Vol. 47, No. 3, 2008, pp. 405–419.

Skillicorn, David B., and Ayron Little, "Patterns of Word Use for Deception in Testimony," *Security Informatics*, Vol. 9, 2010, pp. 25–39.

Slackman, Michael, "Hard-Line Force Extends Grip over a Splintered Iran," *New York Times*, Middle East, July 20, 2009a. As of November 3, 2011:
http://www.nytimes.com/2009/07/21/world/middleeast/21guards.html?_r=1&ref=islamic_revolutionary_guard_corps

———, "Iranian Site Reports a Death Sentence for Protester," *New York Times*, October 9, 2009b.

———, "Tehran Plans to Execute 3 Protesters of Election," *New York Times*, October 11, 2009c.

———, "Iran Guard Commanders Are Killed in Bombings," *New York Times*, Middle East, October 18, 2009d. As of November 3, 2011:
http://www.nytimes.com/2009/10/19/world/middleeast/19iran.html?ref=islamic_revolutionary_guard_corps

———, "Iran Opposition Leaders Drop Demand for New Election," *New York Times*, January 26, 2010a.

———, "Iran Boasts of Capacity to Make Bomb Fuel," *New York Times*, February 12, 2010b.

Slatcher, Richard B., Simine Vazire, and James W. Pennebaker, "Am 'I' More Important Than 'We'? Couples' Word Use in Instant Messages," *Personal Relationships*, Vol. 15, 2008, pp. 407–424.

Stelter, Brian, and Brad Stone, "Stark Images, Uploaded to the World," *New York Times*, June 17, 2009a. As of November 3, 2011:
http://www.nytimes.com/2009/06/18/world/middleeast/18press.html?_r=2

———, "Web Pries Lid of Iranian Censorship," *New York Times*, Middle East, June 22, 2009b. As of November 3, 2011:
http://www.nytimes.com/2009/06/23/world/middleeast/23censor.html?hp

Stirman, Shannon, and James W. Pennebaker, "Word Use in the Poetry of Suicidal and Nonsuicidal Poets," *Psychosomatic Medicine*, Vol. 63, 2001, pp. 517–522.

Stockman, Farah, "US Funds Dry Up for Iran Rights Watchdog," *boston.com, The Boston Globe*, October 6, 2009. As of November 3, 2011:
http://www.boston.com/news/nation/articles/2009/10/06/us_cutoff_of_funding_to_iran_human_rights_cause_signals_shift/?page=full

Stone, Lori D., and James W. Pennebaker, "Trauma in Real Time: Talking and Avoiding Online Conversations About the Death of Princess Diana," *Basic and Applied Social Psychology*, Vol. 24, No. 3, 2002, pp. 173–183.

Tavernise, S., "Pakistan Widens Online Ban to Include YouTube," *New York Times*, May 20, 2010.

Tehrani, Hamid, "Iran's Revolutionary Guards Take on the Internet," Internet and Democracy Blog, January 8, 2009. As of November 3, 2011:
http://blogs.law.harvard.edu/idblog/2009/01/08/irans-revolutionary-guards-take-on-the-internet/

Thaler, David E., Alireza Nader, Shahram Chubin, Jerrold D. Green, Charlotte Lynch, and Frederic Wehrey, *Mullahs, Guards, and Bonyads: An Exploration of Iranian Leadership Dynamics*. Santa Monica, Calif.: RAND Corporation, MG-878-OSD, 2010. As of November 3, 2011:
http://www.rand.org/pubs/monographs/MG878.html

Tompkins, Al, "Iranian Government Uses New Technology to Monitor Information About Political Turmoil," *Poynter*, June 22, 2009. As of November 3, 2011:
http://www.poynter.org/latest-news/als-morning-meeting/96446/
iranian-government-uses-new-technology-to-monitor-information-about-political-turmoil/

TwapperKeeper.com, homepage, no date. As of November 15, 2011:
http://twapperkeeper.com/index.php

Twitter Blog, "Down Time Rescheduled," June 15, 2009a. As of November 3, 2011:
http://blog.twitter.com/2009/06/down-time-rescheduled.html

———, "Top Twitter Trends of 2009," December 15, 2009b. As of November 3, 2011:
http://blog.twitter.com/2009/12/top-twitter-trends-of-2009.html

Twitter Help Center, "What Are Hashtags ("#" Symbols)?" no date. As of November 3, 2011:
http://support.twitter.com/entries/49309-what-are-hashtags-symbols

U.S. Department of State, "Opinion Space: A Universe of Viewpoints and Ideas," website, no date. As of November 3, 2011:
http://www.state.gov/opinionspace/

———, "Department of State Launches New Tool to Foster Online Open Dialogue," March 15, 2010. As of November 3, 2011:
http://www.state.gov/r/pa/prs/ps/2010/03/138326.htm

Warren, Christina, "Iranian Government Bans Gmail," *Mashable*, February 10, 2010. As of November 3, 2011:
http://mashable.com/2010/02/10/iran-bans-gmail/

Wolfowitz, Paul, "Obama Needs to Change Stance on Iran," *Washington Post*, June 19, 2009. As of November 3, 2011:
http://www.washingtonpost.com/wp-dyn/content/article/2009/06/18/
AR2009061803496.html?hpid=opinionsbox1

World Bank, "Iran, Islamic Rep.," no date. As of November 16, 2011:
http://devdata.worldbank.org/ict/irn_ict.pdf

World Bank Group, "Data Profile: Iran, Islamic Rep.," 2010. As of November 3, 2011:
http://ddp-ext.worldbank.org/ext/ddpreports/
ViewSharedReport?&CF=&REPORT_ID=9147&REQUEST_TYPE=VIEWADVANCED

Worth, Robert F., "Despite Warning, Thousands Rally in Iran," *New York Times*, Middle East, September 18, 2009a. As of November 3, 2011:
http://www.nytimes.com/2009/09/19/world/middleeast/19iran.html?bl

———, "Dissidents Mass in Tehran to Subvert an Anti-U.S. Rally," *New York Times*, November 5, 2009b.

Worth, Robert F., and Nazila Fathi, "Iran Gathering Is Broken Up," *New York Times*, July 31, 2009a.

———, "Iranian Students Clash with Police," *New York Times*, December 8, 2009b.

———, "Police Are Said to Have Killed 10 in Iran Protests," *New York Times*, December 29, 2009c.

Worth, Robert F., Nazila Fathi, and Jeff Zeleny, "Despite Warning, Thousands Stage Protests in Iran," *New York Times*, June 22, 2009.

Yusuf, Huma, *Old and New Media: Converging During the Pakistan Emergency (March 2007–February 2008)*, Cambridge, Mass.: Massachusetts Institute of Technology, Center for Future Civic Media, 2009. As of November 3, 2011:
http://civic.mit.edu/blog/humayusuf/old-and-new-media-converging-during-the-pakistan-emergency-march-2007-february-2008

Zeleny, Jeff, "Violence May Hinder Talks with Iran, Obama Says," *New York Times*, Middle East, June 26, 2009. As of November 3, 2011:
http://www.nytimes.com/2009/06/27/world/middleeast/27prexy.html